WALKING WITH MOSES

WALKING
with
MOSES

Forty Lessons from the Life of the Lawgiver

LAWRENCE R. FARLEY

ST·TIKHON'S
MONASTERY
P·R·E·S·S

MMXX

St. Tikhon's Monastery Press, South Canaan, Penn.

Published 2020
PRINTED IN THE UNITED STATES OF AMERICA

ISBN: 978-1-7328522-7-3

Cover Artwork by Hierodeacon Mark
Cover Design by Priest Mikel Hill

Library of Congress Cataloging-in-Publication Data
Names: The Very Reverend Lawrence Farley
Title: Walking with Moses: Forty Lessons from the Life of the Lawgiver
Description: Waymart, Penn.: St. Tikhon's Monastery Press, 2019.
Identifiers: ISBN 978-1-7328522-7-3
Subject: Scripture—Commentary—Eastern Orthodox Christian. Devotion—Eastern Orthodox Christian

Dedicated to the memory of
the Right Reverend H.V.R. Short,
a kind pastor and the best of bishops

TABLE OF CONTENTS

Introduction
Moses the Lawgiver

IT IS EASY FOR MANY CHRISTIANS to ignore Moses. It is true that when Moses is compared to Christ, the Hebrew Lawgiver can only come off poorly. Comparing the Old Covenant to the New Covenant inevitably results in Moses coming in second best, if that. Thus we read in John 1:17, "The Law was given through Moses; grace and truth came through Jesus Christ." Thus also 2 Cor. 3:7–10, which reads, "Now if the ministry of death, carved in letters on stone, was so glorious that the Israelites could not look intently at the face of Moses because of its glory that was going to fade, how much more will the ministry of the Spirit be glorious? For if the ministry of condemnation [i.e., Moses' work] was glorious, the ministry of righteousness will abound much more in glory. Indeed, what was endowed with glory has come to have no glory in this respect because of the glory that surpasses it." Just as some people erroneously believe that the New Testament has rendered the Old Testament texts irrelevant to Christian living, so some others regard Moses as insignificant, as yesterday's man, justly relegated to the sidelines as having little to say to Christians today. He can be safely ignored.[1]

One can understand how this misunderstanding might have arisen. In all New Testament exegesis of the Hebrew Scriptures, Moses and his work are compared to that of Jesus Christ and His work, with the result that Moses' work is judged inferior to it. That is hardly surprising in documents that were intended to convert Jews and persuade them that they should become Christians. But these New Testament documents cannot be read as a complete assessment of Moses, his work, his place in history, and his relevance to Christians—nor were they ever intended to so read. The New Testament writers did not intend to denigrate Moses, or even to offer an objective historical assessment of him and what he did. They only asserted that the glory, achievement, and Law of Moses were never intended by God to be His final word to Israel or to the world. God's final word was not spoken through Moses, but through Jesus Christ. The Law of Moses, though regarded by some in Israel as God's final word, was only preparatory and provisional.

The Law which Moses received on Sinai functioned as a tutor which God gave to His people to bring them to Christ (Gal. 3:24). Christ was central and eternal; the Law was provisional and temporary. Moses' Law was therefore destined to fade from the center stage—but not from our hearts or our theological consideration. Jews might have legitimately said at one time, "We are Moses' disciples" (John 9:28), but eventually Moses stepped down, so that all might become the disciples of Jesus. Yet this does not mean that Moses now has no significance and nothing to teach us. The Fathers, such as St. Gregory of Nyssa, knew this. When asked by his

---

[1]   This belief has a long standing history. Already in the second century A.D.., Marcion (c. 85–160) was promoting the idea that Jesus was in no wise connected with the god of the Old Testament. Modern-day dispensationalists (many Baptists, Pentecostals and non denominationals, among others) hold very similar views regarding the relevance of the Old Testament.

friend Caesarius to instruct him regarding a life of moral perfection, Gregory did not lecture him with abstract concepts, but held up the life of Moses as an example, writing his Life of Moses to offer the great Hebrew Lawgiver as an example to all Christians.

Following in St. Gregory's footsteps, this book looks at the life of the great Moses to see what modern Christians can learn from the life and work of the great Hebrew Lawgiver whose work formed the foundation of the Old Testament. Even a glory that has been eclipsed by a greater glory (see 2 Cor. 3) retains a light that can illumine those in darkness—and darkness has indeed covered the earth and thick darkness the peoples (Isa. 60:2). We can use all the light available to us—even the light which shines from the face of Moses. His experience of the living God when he led his people out of Egypt, through the howling wilderness of Sinai, and to the border of the Promised Land can still offer guidance to us who journey through the howling wilderness of this age, and look for the Promised Land to come.

One final word about the structure of this book. It consists of forty short chapters, brief meditations for the forty days of Lent—either the Great Lent leading to Holy Week and Pascha, or the winter Lent, leading to Christmas. (Of course, it can also be read in several sittings like any other book, if one prefers.) For this reason, each chapter is very short. The chapters refer to the events of Moses' life and comment upon their abiding significance and the lessons one can learn from him, but are not intended to provide anything like a complete exegesis of the text, which is why the Scriptural text itself is not provided. A few exegetical details are provided in the footnotes.

Why speak about Moses during Lent? In the Orthodox Church, in the prayer which the priest says at the conclusion of the Lenten services of the Presanctified Gifts, we read the following:

"O Almighty Master, who in wisdom fashioned all creation, and who through Your ineffable providence and great goodness have led us to these all-revered days for purification of souls and bodies, for restraint of passions, and for the hope of the resurrection, who during the forty days put into the hands of Your servant Moses the tablets of the Law in letters divinely inscribed: grant to us also, O Good One, to fight the good fight, to complete the course of the fast, to preserve the Faith undivided, to crush the heads of invisible serpents, to be shown to be conquerors of sins."

Here, at the heart of our Lenten struggle to achieve sanctity, we find the great Hebrew Lawgiver once again. In this prayer the Church draws a parallel between the forty days which Moses spent on Mount Sinai receiving the Law and the forty days of spiritual exertion which we spend during the fast. During his forty days, Moses received the Law, divinely inscribed by God Himself upon two stone tablets. In our forty days, we hope that God will write His Law upon our very hearts (2 Cor. 3:3). It was Moses' privilege to speak with the living God face to face, as man speaks with his friend (cf. Exod. 33:11), and through this to receive a revelation of the kind of life that God wants for His people. It is the work of Christ, by His All-holy Spirit, to write that revelation in our hearts, and to lead us to a greater transfiguration. We remain grateful to the Lord for all the instruments He uses to accomplish this transfiguring work—including the instrument of His servant Moses. As St. Gregory of Nyssa knew, our struggle to achieve virtue requires a human exemplar. He knew of no better exemplar than Moses. Neither do I.

Part One:

THE HOUSE *of* SLAVERY

Day One
Moses in Egypt: Discovering One's True Family

MOSES AT FIRST HAD NO IDEA who he really was. That is, in a time when one's personal identity was a permanent gift given by one's family (rather than today, when one's identity is changeable and self-made), he did not know who his true family was. Moses was born to a family within the people of Israel, the descendants of Abraham, Isaac, and Jacob, to whom God had promised the Land of Canaan and a glorious destiny. That promise seemingly had proven false, for those descendants were far away from the land promised to them, and furthermore were effectively enslaved in Egypt, the superpower of the day, with no way to leave their shackled existence and find that destiny. Moses was born to a family of the tribe of Levi, an heir, like all of Israel, to the apparently hollow promises of their ancestral God. When the infant emerged from his mother and his newborn cry broke the silent air of the women's quarters where he was born, he had no idea that he had been born into a life of slavery.

Israel, though once favored through their connection with Joseph who served as steward to the mighty Pharaoh in times past, had come down in the world. The people had multiplied in Egypt, and the Egyptians began to perceive this foreign population as a possible threat. If Asiatics invaded from the east (doubtless Egyptian advisors remembered the hegemony of the Hyksos in Egypt),[1] the well-defined, unassimilated Israelites might side with them, with disastrous consequences for the Egyptians. Accordingly, their Egyptian masters treated them as part of the workforce, effectively enslaving them and forcing them to join the corvées that built the storage cities[2] of Pithom and Raamses.[3]

This determination to minimize the internal threat from the foreigners within their midst brought about even worse disasters for the Israelites than their reduction to effective servitude in Egypt. A policy of male genocide was enacted, which required Hebrew midwives to kill the newborns if they were male—doubtless, it was intended, in secret, so that the mothers would think the child was stillborn. By this means it was hoped to limit the male Hebrew population and minimize the number of Hebrew soldiers available in the event of foreign invasion. Fortunately, not all the midwives obeyed this genocidal directive (Exod. 1:15–20). Such was the courage of the women that the text records for posterity the names of two of them: Shiphrah and Puah—which is all the more significant, since the name of Pharaoh was not recorded! Upon the failure of the royal directive to the midwives, a more draconian directive was given: now it was decreed that all male children should be openly destroyed and thrown into the Nile (v. 22).

Thus, Moses was born into a very perilous world. When he

---

1   The Hyksos were part of the great nomadic movement of Semitic peoples from Mesopotamia that became pronounced about 1900 B.C. By about 1720 B.C. they entered into Egypt, and for nearly two centuries they controlled most of the country from their capital at Avaris.

2   The storage cities were attached to temples.

3   If a fifteenth century B.C. date for the Exodus is accepted, the names of the cities must be considered anachronistic—i.e., as names applied at a later date.

was born, his parents[1] saw that he was not sickly, but strong
and healthy, and they could not bear to obey the royal decree.
But keeping him alive was clearly dangerous, for the discovery of his male gender was clear evidence of their defiance of
the Egyptian program to limit the number of Hebrew males.
What then to do?

After three months, when his noisy crying began to be
heard beyond the walls of their dwelling so that the child
could no longer be safely concealed, they decided to place
the child in a wicker container, made waterproof with tar and
pitch, and set him loose in the Nile in hopes of immediate
discovery and adoption by an Egyptian family (Exod. 2:1–
4). The Hebrew word for "container" here is *tebha*, the same
word used the Ark of Noah. Like the Ark, it was a closed-
in container, not an open basket—thus the text speaks of
Pharaoh's daughter "opening it" (v. 6). Just as the hope for
the world's survival depended upon those in the *tebha* made
by Noah, so hope for Israel depended upon the child in the
tebha made by Moses' parents. Such a strategy was not novel.[2]

The baby was found by Pharaoh's daughter who went
down with her retinue to bathe in the Nile. She immediately
recognized the child as one of the Hebrews. Her heart went
out to the baby when it began to cry (Exod. 2:6),[3] and she re-
solved to keep the child. Moses' sister, who had been watch-

---

1 The Exodus narrative here leaves them unnamed (as it does Pharaoh and his daughter) to allow the spotlight to fall exclusively
   upon Moses.

2 An 800 B.C. story, the Legend of Sargon's Birth, relates that Sargon, the founder of the dynasty of Akkad in the twenty-fourth
   century B.C., had been hid in a basket in the Euphrates River. In a
   Hittite myth, a royal mother gives birth to thirty sons, places them
   in caulked baskets, and sends them down a river. Evidently the
   concept of saving children in this way was something of a cultural
   commonplace, though this in no wise suggests that the episode recorded in Exodus was fictitious.

3 Thus the word "behold!": "When she opened it, she saw the child,
   and behold!—a boy was crying."

ing the events unfold, immediately approached and volunteered to find a wet nurse for the child. She of course went to find her mother who was chosen as the wet nurse and was given the appropriate wages for her employment by the royal household. The Scriptural narrative delights to point out the happy irony of the Hebrew mother taking money from the Egyptians to nurse her own child!

Pharaoh's daughter named the child "Moses." The Hebrew narrator points out the connection of the name (*Mosheh* in Hebrew) with the Hebrew verb for "to draw" (*mashah*), saying that the name was chosen because Pharaoh's daughter "drew" him out of the water. This is true enough, and it serves to make the name which the Egyptian woman gave to Moses acceptable to the Hebrews.

In fact, Pharaoh's daughter was not thinking of the Hebrew word for "to draw," but gave the newborn a thoroughly Egyptian name, as one might expect. The name "Mosheh"—Egyptian ms(w)—means "begets" or "a son" in Egyptian and formed a part of such Egyptian names as "Thutmosis"—i.e., "Thoth begets", or "son of Thoth." The etymological coincidence of the Hebrew word *mashah* with the Egyptian word ms(w) serves to make the child a true Hebrew for the readers of the narrative, rather than a foreign interloper. It also fitly expresses the child's dual heritage—he is both Hebrew and Egyptian, born to a Levite and raised by Pharaoh's daughter as part of the extended royal household.

In the Exodus narrative, we next see the newborn as a grown man. The text reads, "Now it came about in those days, when Moses had grown up, that he went out to his brethren and looked on their burdens; and he saw an Egyptian beating a Hebrew, one of his brethren" (Exod. 2:11). This short verse omits a multitude of biographical details, skipping over them to focus upon the narrative's main theme, which is not the life of Moses, but the redeeming love of Israel's God. It is certain that being raised in the royal house meant that Moses would have received a thorough training, "educated in all the learning of the Egyptians" (Acts 7:22). This would have included training in literature, scribal arts, rhetoric, and warfare—skills which would all be useful in his future role as Lawgiver and leader. He would also have been trained in foreign languages.

It is apparent that by the time Moses had grown to adulthood, he had also become aware of his Hebrew heritage. This is why we find mention of "his brethren" twice in such a short verse. How he became aware of it—fascinating as such a story would be to us (and to filmmakers) —we are not told. But it seems that his zeal to avenge the oppression of the Hebrews in Egypt went beyond a mere concern for social justice. Rather, Moses identified personally with the Hebrews in their affliction—an identification doubtless made all the keener by the fact that as an Egyptian from the royal house he was exempt from experiencing such affliction personally. As a member of the privileged elite, he doubtless felt that he was in a position to intervene, avenge, and correct such injustices. That was why, when he saw an Egyptian beating one of his fellow countrymen (probably one of the captains of the laborgangs), he reacted with violence, striking him dead.

It is probable that Moses did not actually intend to kill the man, and that his death was accidental. But the killing of an Egyptian taskmaster by a Hebrew—even one of the royal house—was too great an offense to be simply ignored. Moses therefore attempted to conceal his sin by burying the corpse in the sand.

Sins are not so easily concealed. The very next day, when Moses saw two Hebrews quarreling and attempted to intervene and reconcile them, one turned on him, and demanded, "Who made you a prince or a judge over us? Are you intending to kill me, as you killed the Egyptian?" (Exod. 2:14). One imagines that the Hebrew responded to Moses in this way because he resented Moses' privileged position. Moses was part of the oppressing elite, one who had never done a day's work in his life (as the man thought)—who did he think he was assuming he could boss around the other Hebrews?

Moses, already reeling internally from the blows of his guilty conscience, responded with panic.[1] He assumed that the matter had become generally known within a mere day, and that retribution would soon follow. Indeed, given the Egyptians' ethnic pride, it was a great crime for a foreigner to kill an Egyptian. It is arguable that the privileges Moses received by being raised in the royal house would make his crime all the more heinous in Egyptian eyes. Indeed, when news reached Pharaoh, the wheels were set in motion which could only result in Moses' execution for his crime.

Moses therefore fled from Egypt, heading far to the east, in the land of Midian (in this case, in northwestern Arabia). He settled in that land, far from Egypt, far from the injustices he saw which caused him such grief, far from his people. And, the sacred text relates, preparing for the next step in the story, "he sat down[2] by a well" (Exod. 2:15), ready to make a new life for himself in a new land.

— *Lessons from the Lawgiver's Life*

What lessons can we learn from these events in the life of Moses? We mention three of them:

1   Heb. 11:27 says, "By faith he left Egypt, not fearing the wrath of the king; for he endured, as seeing Him who is unseen." This should not be read as contradicting the Exodus account (which clearly says that Moses did fear the wrath of Pharaoh), but as a further and deeper reflection on his flight. The point was that Moses did not turn his back forever on his people when he left Egypt (which one solely motivated by a sense of self-preservation would do), but left room in his heart for a future return, enduring whatever befell him as he trusted in God.

2   In Hebrew this involves a play on words: Moses "settled [Hebrew *yashab*] in the land of Midian, and he sat down [Hebrew *yashab*] by a well." Moses' settled life there thus began after he sat down by a well, since the events occurring at the well resulted in his taking a wife and becoming part of an extended Midianite family.

First of all, no knowledge is to be despised. The New Testament records that Moses was educated in all the learning of the Egyptians (Acts 7:22) without a whisper of reproof, despite the fact that such education also involved the worship of the Egyptian gods. Christians need not fear higher education and should not retreat into fundamentalist ghettoized enclaves out of fear that such learning may contaminate them. This has always been the attitude of the Church: St. Basil famously encouraged secular learning in his day, despite the fact that such learning involved stories of the pagan gods who were still worshiped by many in society. All truth is God's truth, and therefore may be claimed by Christians as theirs as well. As St. Justin Martyr said, "Whatever things were rightly said among all men are the property of us Christians."[1] Truth may be mixed in with error, but a godly discernment will know how to sift it out, learning and claiming what is good, while leaving the bad to one side.

Secondly, spiritual growth depends upon recognizing one's true family. Though Moses was raised among Egyptians and doubtless came to love the family in which he was raised, a time came when he had to recognize that they were not his true family and to make solidarity with the Hebrews his primary loyalty. It is the same with Christians in this dark and dangerous time: though we love and value family, tribe, race, and country, our true family consists of fellow Christians, whatever their tribe, race, or country.

Sometimes the choice can be stark and heartbreaking, such as when our biological family opposes our Christian faith and demands that we choose family loyalty over loyalty to Christ. Then the word of the Lord calls us to choose: "If anyone comes to Me and does not hate[2] his own father and mother and wife and children and brothers and sisters,

---

1   The *Second Apology*, chapter 13.
2   The word "hate" here means "reject"; it refers to a choice, not an emotion.

yes, and even his own life, he cannot be My disciple" (Luke
14:26). When a biological family is united in their worship
of Christ, such terrible choices do not come into play. But
even then we know that loyalty to Christ supersedes every
other loyalty—including a patriotic loyalty to one's country.
In countries such as America which place a high value on pa-
triotism and national loyalty, one is tempted to say, "This is
a hard saying; who can hear it?" (Cf. John 6:60). But it remains true nonetheless. Despite Moses' love for the woman
and family which reared him, nurtured him, protected him,
educated him, and gave him all the advantages which came
with membership in the royal family, he still needed to turn
against them, and side with his true Hebrew family.

Finally, we learn from Moses' actions that human zeal
alone cannot accomplish the work of God. Moses was right
in believing that his people were being unjustly oppressed
by their Egyptian overlords, and in desiring their liberation.
He was wrong in supposing that their liberation could come
about through human effort alone. Striking the Egyptian
taskmaster and trying to unite Israel around him on the basis
of his political importance and his connections with the royal family were ill-considered and futile. Mere unaided human
effort can never fulfill God's purposes.

Abraham learned this many years before Moses: God had
promised him that his descendants would be as numerous as
the dust of the earth (Gen. 13:16), and when it was clear that
he could not have a son through his wife Sarah, at Sarah's
suggestion, he took matters into his own hands to have a son
through his concubine Hagar. It seemed reasonable enough,
for the child born of Hagar would still be legally his son. But
such human effort was not the way to fulfill God's purposes. Though the child of Hagar was to enjoy God's blessing
(Gen. 17:20), God's promise to Abraham would be fulfilled
through God's miraculous work in Sarah and through the
child that Sarah bore him. Unaided human zeal alone is always insufficient in the Kingdom of God. Christians must

always depend upon God as they work to advance His cause. In all our effort we must remember that it is "Not by might, nor by power, but by My Spirit, says the Lord of Hosts" (Zech. 4:6).

Day Two
Moses in Midian: Settling Down in Peace

MOSES' FLIGHT FROM EGYPT to Midian is related laconically enough: "Moses fled from the face of Pharaoh and settled in the land of Midian" (Exod. 2:15). The narrator does not comment on Moses' state of mind, but we may well imagine that he was discouraged and depressed with his utter failure to galvanize and liberate his Hebrew countrymen, and his forced exile from the family he loved and with whom he had grown to manhood. Though he embraced his Hebrew lineage and identified with the Hebrews in the plight, he was still very much an Egyptian—one who had been forced to leave the homeland he loved.

This is apparent from the first story told upon his arrival in Midian. He was sitting by the community well, when the seven daughters of a local priest came to the well to perform the arduous work of drawing water for their father's flocks. The work of shepherding was men's work, and the fact that the girls were doing this indicated that they had no brothers—brothers who could protect them from local bullies. The local bullies—other shepherds—therefore came to drive them away, presumably to use the well first.

With the same kind of physical courage in the face of unjust aggression that Moses displayed in Egypt (Exod. 2:11–12), he stood up to the bullies, and even helped the girls water their flocks by drawing the water for them. He did not insist on thanks for his gallantry; he apparently took for granted that such heroism and self-sacrifice were his duty. The girls then simply returned to their father and related to him what had happened.

In their recounting of the story, Moses was "an Egyptian" who "delivered us from the hand of the shepherds."[1] Note that Moses looked like who he was—not a Hebrew, but an Egyptian. Moreover, the Egyptian did not just save them from the bullies but took the extra and extraordinary step of watering their flock for them. The sacred code of hospitality demanded that such acts of gallantry be rewarded. The father, Reuel by name,[2] therefore sent them back to the scene of their rescue to invite the stranger home for a meal.

The meal was the beginning of a long association with this new family in Midian, for eventually Moses married one of the girls, Zipporah (presumably the eldest). For the third time the narrator uses the Hebrew verb *yashab* (see the previous footnote on verse 15), saying, "And Moses agreed to dwell [*yashab*] with the man, and he gave his daughter Zipporah to Moses" (Exod. 2:21). The repetition of this verb expresses this new phase of Moses' life. He was a Hebrew by birth, and an Egyptian by upbringing, education, and appearance. Now he became a Midianite and joined their tribe. The text says that Moses "agreed" (Hebrew *yaal*), indicating that Reuel made him an offer of one of the girls in marriage, suggesting that Moses settle among them. It was to this offer that Moses "agreed."

---

1   We pause to note the definite article: "the shepherds." It is likely that these bullies were well-known to them, and that this was not the first time they had been subjected to such harassment.

2   In Exod. 3:1 and Num. 10:29 Moses' father-in-law is referred to as "Jethro," not "Reuel." It seems that Reuel was the patriarch or "father" of the clan, but that Jethro was the actual father of the girls. Some commentators suggest that "Reuel" was Jethro's clan name, but there is no indication in the text that Reuel and Jethro were the same person.

Thenceforth Moses would dwell [*yashab*] in Midian as his new home and settle down to a life far from the pain he knew in Egypt. It promised to be a good life: his wife soon gave birth to a son (an obvious blessing in a culture which valued boys over girls). In a poignant nod to his former life, he named the boy "Gershom," saying, "I have been a sojourner [Hebrew *ger*], in a foreign land."[1] Midian was now his home, even if it was for him a foreign land, far from his native Egypt.

It was during the performance of duties in this new life that God called upon Moses. Shepherding was men's work, and so Moses took over the task of head shepherd. He was shepherding his father-in-law Jethro's[2] flock far away from his home in Midian.[3] Moses "led the flock to the west side of the wilderness, and came to Horeb,"[4] to the place that would be afterward hallowed as "the mountain of God" (Exod. 3:1). Moses did not know it, but as he was making a new life for himself in Midian, things had become worse for his countrymen in Egypt, and they cried out to God, "and their cry for help from their slavery rose up to God" and "God heard their groaning, and God remembered His covenant with Abraham, Isaac, and Jacob" (Exod. 2:23–24). Moses' life was about the change.

---

1   The connection of the words *ger* [Hebrew for "sojourner"] and sham [Hebrew for "there"] with the name "Gershom" was a popular etymology, suggested by a likeness of the sounds. In fact the name "Gershom" was already in use then, and was derived from the Hebrew verb *garash*.

2   Now that Moses was married, his primary connection with the Midian clan was no longer with Reuel, but with Jethro, the father of his wife.

3   Such distances were not unusual for shepherds in that time, and there is no warrant to locate Horeb in Midian, as some have attempted to do. By way of comparison, Jacob sent Joseph to check on his flocks and he went 56 miles to the north, only to discover that they were another 15 miles away (Gen. 37:14ff.).

4   It would seem that "Horeb" denoted the wilderness in which the mountain of God—called "Sinai" was found. The name "Horeb" means "dry wasteland."

— Lessons from the Lawgiver's Life

Moses' life in Midian and his decision to settle down in peace there (as indicated by his beginning a family and the name he gave to his new son) provides the classic example of the aphorism, "Man proposes, but God disposes." Moses had decided that he was an Egyptian no longer, and that the suffering of his ancestral people was no longer his concern, for he could clearly do nothing about it. He would leave Egypt to Pharaoh and Israel to God, and raise his family in Midian, far from the turmoil that once characterized his life. But God decided otherwise, as Moses would soon discover.

This teaches us that we may make plans to the best of our ability and wisdom but must always leave room for the hand of God. St. Philaret, Metropolitan of Moscow, knew this too, as we read in the prayer he composed and which many Orthodox prayer books contain: "Teach me to treat whatever may happen to me throughout the day with peace of soul and with firm conviction that Your will governs all. In unforeseen events, let me not forget that all is sent by You." We may make our plans, but all of them must be contingent, knowing that all things are in the hand of God. It is as St. James wrote: "You do not know what your life will be like tomorrow. You are a vapor that appears for a little while and then vanishes away. Instead, say, 'If the Lord wills, we will live, and also do this or that'" (James 4:14–15). We are all beggars at God's table, dependent upon Him for life, breath, food, and all that we possess—indeed, we are just a vapor that appears for a little while and then vanishes away. The contingency of our plans reflects the fragility of our existence.

Moses' actions in Midian also teach us that we are our brothers' (and sisters') keeper. He could have ignored the plight of the seven Midianite girls who were being bullied by the shepherds. He could have decided that it was not his business, and that it would be prudent not to begin his sojourn in a foreign land by antagonizing the menfolk of the village (i.e., the shepherds). He might have decided to make peaceful coexistence with everyone minding his own business, his watchword. But he decided otherwise and stood up to the local bullies. His gallantry and bravery (he was, after all, outnumbered) was justly repaid. His actions challenge us also to step into the breach whenever we see injustice being done before our faces. We must not be foolhardy in our actions, but neither may we may cowardly in our inaction. The daughters of Reuel and their bullies are still all around us and call us to action.

Day Three
Moses in Midian: The Burning Bush

A S MOSES PASTURED his father-in-law's flock, he came upon an amazing sight: a bush was burning, yet its foliage was not consumed. He therefore "turned aside," distracted by this supernatural sight, and drew near to get a better look at this spectacle (Exod. 3:3).[1] But why did God choose such a sign as a way of getting Moses' attention? Admittedly, apart from such small bushes, there was not much else in the wilderness of Horeb except rocks, and rocks are dead and do not burn. But the sign of a living bush aflame with a fire which did not consume it was apt, because this was precisely the goal which God had for His people. God was a consuming fire, burning up sin and impurity. But how could a sinful people have such a One living in their midst? "Who among us can live with the consuming fire? Who among us can live with eternal burning?" (Isa. 33:14). How could sinful Israel draw near to the Holy One without being consumed?

The Law, with its provision for tabernacle, altar, priesthood, and laws for the required purifications, gives the answer. By keeping God's Law and serving Him in humble faith,

---

[1] The Hebrew text stresses Moses' fascination with the sight by using the Hebrew verb *ra'ah*, "to see" seven times in six verses to describe the actions of Yahweh and Moses.

and by drawing near to Him as He instructed, sinful Israel could safely have the Holy One dwelling in their midst. Moses would receive instructions on Mount Sinai which would enable the bush to burn with the presence of the holy God, and still not be consumed.[1] Israel was the living bush, and God in their midst the consuming fire.

The miraculously burning bush was God's summons to His servant Moses, and when it got his attention, God called him: "Moses, Moses!", inviting him to come closer.[2] Moses responded with an open heart: "and he said, "Here I am" (v. 4). God first demanded that he remove his sandals from his feet, since priests entered a temple barefoot to serve their god. This demand concealed a secret: wherever God revealed Himself was holy ground. Moses saw no temple, but even so this patch of soil on Horeb was holy because God revealed Himself there. Pagan gods were found in their immovable temples, but this God could reveal Himself anywhere.[3]

And He revealed Himself not only as the ancestral God of his fathers, the God of Abraham, Isaac, and Jacob, but as the God of their descendants who were even then suffering in Egypt—that is, as the God of the people whom Moses had abandoned. He declared that He was now going to rescue them from their affliction and fulfill His ancient promise to

---

1   Later Christian reflection which knew God dwelling among men through the Incarnation would come to discern in the burning bush a prefiguration of Mary, in whose womb dwelt the divine Word. The eternal fire dwelt in her also, and yet she was not consumed.

2   The repetition of the name is a token of endearment as well as urgency; compare 1 Sam. 3:10; Luke 10:41; and Acts 9:4.

3   Thus Exod. 3:2 identifies the speaker as "the angel of Yahweh," identified in v. 4ff. as Yahweh Himself. The term "the angel of Yahweh" here does not refer to one the created messengers of God (such as in Ps. 103:20). The term "angel" or "messenger" [Hebrew mal'ak] was used in such contexts to show that Yahweh's presence was not confined to a particular shrine or locale, as were pagan gods.

bring them all into a "good and spacious land, a land flowing with milk and honey" (v. 8) (i.e., to a land in which they as a pastoral–nomadic people could find prosperity). To Moses' surprise, He also said that He would send him, Moses, to bring them out of Egypt to inherit this good land.

That must have seemed to Moses like an absurd plan. He had already proved himself spectacularly unequal to this task, which is why he was dwelling in Midian, and not in Egypt. Moses therefore asked the obvious, asking, "Who am I that I should go to Pharaoh, and that I should bring the sons of Israel out of Egypt?" (v. 11). God seemed oblivious to the obvious, and simply replied that He would be with him, and that when he had brought Israel out of Egypt to this mountain in Horeb, it would serve as a sign of His power.

Moses continued to protest. He had failed to galvanize Israel or convince them of his authority to lead before. Why should they believe him now? If he said that the God of their fathers had sent him to lead them, what evidence could he present them with? If they asked for His Name, what should he tell them?

We must remember that in ancient times a name was not simply a verbal designation or label, but a reputation built on the basis of one's deeds. A god's "name" was the assertion of his power, his earned status. The request for God's "Name" therefore was a request for proof that God could save Israel from their seemingly impossible situation.

In answer, God replied, "I am whom I am; thus you shall say to the sons of Israel: I Am has sent me to you" (Exod. 3:14). The verb "I am," or "to be," is the Hebrew *hayah*; the Divine Name Yahweh was based upon that verb. In referring to Himself as Yahweh, the great "I Am," God was declaring that He was limited by no one, that He could do whatever He willed—including bringing Israel out of Egypt. The NAME "Yahweh" was not new to Israel; Abraham had worshiped God using that name (for example, see Gen. 15:2, where Abraham addresses God as "Lord Yahweh"). It is unlikely that they had somehow forgotten the name through the centuries—would they not repeat the name every time they prayed?

God was not revealing a new verbal tag, but a hitherto unseen power to save. He was declaring to Moses and Israel His ability to do whatever He willed—including the salvation of Israel, however hopeless it seemed. He was not just the God of Abraham, Isaac, and Jacob, but the hope of the hopeless, and the one who could rescue His people from the iron furnace, the house of slavery. All of Pharaoh's might was nothing before Him. God warned Moses that Pharaoh would not instantly comply but would only do so when forced by God after Egypt had been struck over and over again. Pharaoh would harden his heart and refuse Moses' demands. He would only relent after the great I Am had manifested His power in the midst of Egypt.

Moses remained unconvinced, perhaps because he keenly felt his own (proven) inadequacy for the task. How could he persuade Israel to follow him, given his reputation as a failure and a fugitive? Before, he was part of the royal household; now he was only a simple shepherd. In response, God asked, "What is that in your hand?" (Exod. 4:2). It was, of course, Moses' shepherd's staff, since he was a shepherd—the very sign of his humble position, his weakness, and his inadequacy. Moses, being a mere man, carried a staff, as did all men in that day. God commanded Moses to "throw it on the ground"—whereupon it became a serpent, so that Moses fled in fear from it! Upon grasping it by the tail at God's further command—something Moses only did because he was so instructed, for grasping a snake by its tail was a sure way to be bit—it became a harmless staff again. The staff of Moses would feature throughout the narrative of Moses' life, and serve as the instrument of divine salvation. Moses' weakness and humility, imaged by his staff, was the channel through which God's power was to be made known.

There was more. Putting his hand into his bosom resulted

in it become white with leprosy[1]—and then, upon doing it a second time, instantly whole again. To these two signs God added a third, which could only be performed in Egypt: if these signs were insufficient, Moses could pour water from the Nile on the ground and it would become blood.

What did these signs mean? They were not intended simply as wonders, or miracles to make men gape. They were also revelations that it was the God of the enslaved Hebrews who was sovereign over Egypt, not Pharaoh or the gods of Egypt. The serpent was an image of Egyptian power, and Pharaoh wore such an image on his crown. But Moses' God had power to nullify this power, so that Pharaoh's terrifying might could do no more harm than a wooden staff could do. It was Yahweh, the God of Israel, who had the power of life and death, to smite and to heal, as the leprous hand and its healing also testified. It was Yahweh who could triumph over the gods of Egypt, who were powerless before Him. The Nile was thought to be divine, a source of life for the Egyptians, but the God of the despised Hebrews could turn their life into death if He willed. None could withstand Him—and His demands for the liberation of His people must therefore be instantly granted. The signs were proof that Yahweh had power to liberate Israel, and moreover, that Moses had truly been sent by Him.

As Moses felt increasingly that his reasons for refusing the call were slipping away, he protested (absurdly for one educated in the royal house) that he was not eloquent enough or experienced enough diplomatically to speak to Pharaoh on the international stage, that he was a man "slow of speech and slow of tongue" (Exod. 4:10). God simply disallowed the protest, saying that He who made a man's tongue could make Moses eloquent enough. In desperation, Moses finally simply attempted to refuse the call, imploring God, "Please,

---

[1]   Leprosy here means not necessarily "Hansen's disease," but any infectious skin condition.

Lord, send the message by whoever You will"—i.e., "by anyone but me," though of course this last detail of defiant refusal was left unstated (v. 13).

This was daring to the point of impiety, and God's patience was at an end: "The anger of Yahweh burned against
Moses." There would be no further discussion or haggling;
Moses was to go to Egypt. Yet even here God had mercy on
His trembling servant. Instead of simply ordering Moses to
do what he was told, he allowed him to work with his brother Aaron, who would serve as his mouthpiece. Throughout
all this exchange the emphasis falls on the importance of the
message God was to give to Pharaoh, for the word "mouth" is
used seven times in as many verses.

— *Lessons from the Lawgiver's Life*

Moses stood before God in weakness at the burning bush.
His attempts to rescue, galvanize, and liberate his ancestral people from their plight had come to nothing, and the
young prince from the royal house now lived the life of a
humble shepherd in faraway Midian, shepherding his father-
in-law's flock. The staff in his hand was a visible symbol of his
weakness and his humble position. But it was just this piece
of wood that God chose to be the instrument of His divine
power. Through the humble staff of a shepherd God would
humiliate Pharaoh and liberate His people. Yahweh was Israel's true shepherd, and He would lead them out from a slave's
labors to the waters of rest. Moses' staff would become God's
staff, and Moses' weakness the instrument of His power.

Moses' wooden staff prefigured another piece of wood—
that of the cross of the Christ. The cross was a symbol of the
weakness of Christ before the powers of this age. Christ commanded no army, had no access to wealth or worldly power.
He had no place to lay His head, and when He died He had
been despoiled even of the clothes on His back. As St. Paul
said, "He was crucified because of weakness" (2 Cor. 13:4).

Yet His cross became the power of God for salvation (1 Cor. 1:18), the invincible trophy, the weapon of peace.[1] The weak things of the world, when offered to God, become strong.

It is the same for Christians, those who have taken up the cross to follow Christ. We also are present in this world as powerless and weak—in many places in the world, as a persecuted minority, as sheep to be slaughtered (cf. Ps. 44:22; Rom. 8:36). Our weakness shows that we carry the treasure of God within us as in earthen vessels, and that the glory for our survival and ultimate triumph belongs to God. We should not be ashamed of our humble position in the world. We should rather embrace it and allow God's glory to shine through our weakness. As St. Paul discovered after he besought the Lord three times to remove a source of affliction, Christ's power is made perfect through our weakness (2 Cor. 12:9).

---

1   From the *kontakion* of the Feast of the Exaltation of the Cross.

Day Four

Leaving Midian for Egypt

MOSES THEREFORE RETURNED to Jethro in Midian to ask for his blessing to leave home and relocate in Egypt. Significantly, he did not tell Jethro what God had said to him, nor that he was planning to confront Pharaoh and lead an independence movement which would bring Israel out of Egypt. Omitting these details was prudent, for it was unlikely that Jethro would have given his blessing to bring his daughter and grandchildren into such a dangerous situation! Instead Moses said that he wanted to return to Egypt to see if his family there was still alive. To this project, Jethro gave his blessing, and Moses returned to Egypt with his wife and sons.[1] God also added His assurance, revealing to Moses that those who sought to execute him were dead, and relocation to Egypt would not in itself endanger his life or the life of his family. Only after this assurance did Moses decide to bring his family with him.

The relocation of the entire family is narrated to stress the finality of Moses' break with Midian, and his determination to embrace his new destiny. He did not leave his family behind to wait for him in case his mission in Egypt didn't work

---

1   Note the plural; until now only the birth of the first born, Gershom, had been narrated. 1 Chron. 23:15 relates that a second son, Eliezer, had also been born to him.

out and he had to return to resume his quiet life in Midian. They went as a family, so that Moses could fulfill the will of Yahweh.[1] The text makes explicit that as he left Midian, "Moses also took the staff of God in his hand" (Exod. 4:20)—i.e., he departed from his home under orders from God, and intent on obeying them.

On the long journey from Midian to Egypt, Scripture narrates two other events. These serve to reveal how Moses was prepared for his task in Egypt, and to set the stage for the confrontations that would come after.

The first event occurred at a lodging place, an oasis between Midian and Egypt, where Moses suffered a bout of sickness which threatened to take his life.[2] His wife Zipporah took immediate action, and circumcised her son, touching (or dropping) the foreskin on Moses' "feet" (i.e., his genitals; compare the euphemisms in Deut. 28:57, Isa. 7:20, Ezek. 16:25),[3] saying, "You are indeed a bridegroom of blood to me!" referring to "the blood of the circumcised"[4] (Exod. 4:26).

Much ink has been spilled on these few verses, with almost all of its sparse details subjected to varying interpretations. I suggest that in Exod. 4:24 the "him" whom Yahweh sought

---

1   The next time we hear of Zipporah is in Exod. 18:2 where she was back in Midian with her father Jethro. It seems that when things became dangerous for Moses during his confrontations with Pharaoh, Moses sent his family back to the safety of Midian.

2   Hebrew thought ascribed all causality to God, and thus the text says, "Yahweh met him and sought to kill him" (Exod. 4:24)—i.e., he suffered a near-fatal attack. The nature of the illness is not specified.

3   It is possible that the reference to Moses' genitals here indicates that Moses had not been properly circumcised (the Egyptians practiced only a partial circumcision) and by that act Zipporah was saying, "Let the one circumcision take the place of the other."

4   This word ("circumcised") is in the plural, referring to all the circumcised people of Israel whom Gershom (and by extension Moses) had now joined.

to slay was Moses, the antecedent of the previous verses. Zipporah's son whom she circumcised in v. 25 was Gershom, the only son of Moses and Zipporah previously named (Exod. 2:22). The question arises, however, why Moses did not circumcise his children before this. Midianites did not circumcise their boys on the eighth day, as God required Abraham's descendants to do. The Midianites circumcised their male children on their entry into manhood, and since Moses and his children were now Midianites, it makes sense that his children's circumcision would have been deferred.

As Moses journeyed into Egypt to lead the Hebrew people, his obedience to the covenant which God made with them was deemed essential, including the requirement of circumcision on the eighth day. The sickness which threatened Moses' life was given as a warning that he must now faithfully fulfill the requirements of his ancestral people. Zipporah was shrewd enough to realize this and took the appropriate action. Her declaration that now he was a blood-bridegroom was her boast that she had saved his life through this circumcision. He was therefore doubly bound to her as her bridegroom, since she saved his life through the blood of the circumcision of their first born.

This episode has further significance, for it follows God's instruction to Moses that he insist that Pharaoh release Israel as His first born son, and that Pharaoh's refusal to do so would result in God's killing the firstborn of Egypt. That Moses had been saved from death by the circumcised blood of his firstborn foreshadowed the salvation of the Israelites in Egypt because they were the circumcised people of God on the night when all the firstborn of the Egyptians were killed. Moses discovered on his way to Egypt that circumcision (i.e., being part of the covenant people of God) delivers from death.

The second event on the way from Midian to Egypt involved Moses' brother Aaron. God reassured Moses that Aaron would gladly help him and serve as his mouthpiece in this seemingly impossible mission to Pharaoh. Accordingly, God sent Aaron from his home in Egypt to Horeb to meet Moses there, and when they met, Aaron indeed greeted his brother Moses and agreed to do all that Moses asked. This was, in fact, a remarkable sign and confirmation of God's promise to give success. The project of liberating Israel from Egypt seemed so fantastic and impossible that no one could possibly agree to such a mad scheme. Yet Aaron instantly agreed to it, and together Moses and Aaron journeyed back to Egypt. Moses' life in Midian was over. His life's work in Egypt and Sinai was about to begin.

— *Lessons from the Lawgiver's Life*

Like all who serve God in truth, Moses was keenly aware of his sins, his failures, his brokenness, and his inadequacy. Indeed, an overwhelming confidence in one's ability and sanctity is never a good sign, but usually a warning of the cancerous growth of fatal and deluding pride. Eyes that are open and hearts that are true will recognize that if we rely upon our own strength, we can do nothing, and that our all adequacy for a task comes from God (John 15:5, 2 Cor. 3:5).

Moses therefore feared to accept God's summons, not because he feared the wrath of Pharaoh (Heb. 11:27), but because failing in this task would be catastrophic for his ancestral people. The lesson he learned as he stood in the illumining glow of the burning bush was that all our adequacy for spiritual work comes from God, and that He will supply the power we need to do the work to which He calls us. To the question, "Who am I that I should go to Pharaoh?" comes the answer, "I will be with you" (Exod. 3:11–12). We must therefore never look to the difficulty of the task God assigns us, or to our own weakness—only to God and His power to work through us. We remain but earthen vessels, fragile, and easily shattered. The surpassing greatness of the power belongs to God alone (2 Cor. 4:7).

Further, we learn the lesson that spiritual warfare (whether the war against Pharaoh or the demons) cannot be combined with disobedience to God. Moses was about to enter into the Egyptian arena of conflict, and so he needed to obey God's commandment regarding circumcision. In the same way, if we are to engage in spiritual conflict with the unseen powers (Eph. 6:12ff.), we also need to repent of all known sin and walk in obedience to His commandments. Refusal to fight against known sin allows the Enemy to make a beachhead in our souls, and in the arena of spiritual warfare, such enemy beachheads can lead to terrible and catastrophic results. The Enemy of our souls is quick to exploit any weakness that can be found in us. The path that leads to life—and spiritual victory—the straight and narrow way of keeping God's commandments.

Finally, we learn the lesson that we need help from others who possess the gifts that we do not. In His patience God joined Aaron to Moses, allowing Aaron to function as Moses' mouthpiece. We see this principle of cooperation at work par excellence in the Church, where each person has his or her own specific gift which they offer for the common good. Just as different members of the human body have different functions in that body, so different Christians have differing gifts and tasks in the Church. Not all can speak eloquently, and not all possess gifts of insight. But each one has been given a gift by God, and the Body of Christ needs all these gifts if it is to function properly. Moses needed Aaron, and we all need each other. Our mutual need of each other's gifts shows that all our power ultimately comes from God alone.

Day Five
The Return to Egypt: Defying Pharaoh

The Audience with Pharaoh

THE NARRATIVE IN EXODUS continues with the words, "Then Moses and Aaron went and assembled all the elders of the sons of Israel, and Aaron [as Moses' spokesman] spoke all the words which Yahweh had spoken to Moses. He then performed the signs in the sight of the people" (Exod. 4:29–30)—i.e., the signs of the staff becoming a serpent, and of the leprosy and healing of Moses' hand.[1] The people believed Moses and Aaron, and expressed their support of Moses' leadership by bowing low and worshipping (v. 31), prostrating themselves before them in acknowledgment that Yahweh had called them to bring them out of Egypt. Thus it was that as the representatives of the Hebrews, Moses and Aaron sought an audience with Pharaoh.

It was Pharaoh's role as king to give justice to the oppressed of his people. Moses' demand for justice as Yahweh's plenipotentiary was plain and to the point: "Thus says Yahweh, the God of Israel: 'Let My people go that they may cel-

---

1   Possibly the third sign of the Nile water becoming blood was not required; Yahweh added it only as a provision "if they will not believe the two signs" (Exod. 4:9).

ebrate a feast to Me in the wilderness'" (Exod. 5:1). Moses did not speak on behalf of Israel, but of Israel's God, who demanded that Pharaoh release His people so that they could leave Egypt to keep a feast to Him in the wilderness, far from Egypt. (We recall the original version of this demand related in Exod. 3:18: "Say to [Pharaoh], 'Yahweh, the God of the Hebrews has met with us [i.e., through the theophany to Moses at the burning bush]. So now please let us go a three days' journey into the wilderness that we may sacrifice to Yahweh our God'".)

The reference to a "three days' journey" was a verbal convention of Near Eastern bargaining, a way of eventually asking for them to depart to a place far from Egypt—i.e., to a place far enough that they would not return. Pharaoh of course understood the convention and what Moses was actually proposing, and categorically refused the demand—as Yahweh had said that he would. Pharaoh was a murderous oppressor of Israel who dealt with them with a hardened heart. God declared that He would now harden Pharaoh's heart so that he would perversely refuse to let Israel go, despite the many blows God inflicted upon Egypt as a judgment for Pharaoh's hard-hearted oppression of His people.[1]

Pharaoh was unimpressed by Moses' demand. Yahweh was not one of the gods he worshiped ("I do not know Yahweh"), and he refused to let Israel go. After this, Moses' then spoke not as Yahweh's representative, but as the representative of the Hebrews, and he repeated the request that Israel be released to journey away from Egypt for three days (i.e., to

---

1   This hardening of Pharaoh's heart by God must be understood in the cultural context of its time, in which all human events were viewed as somehow caused by God: thus Exod. 21:13; Deut. 2:30; 1 Sam. 1:5; 2:25. One misreads the text if one regards Pharaoh as the helpless victim whose heart God arbitrarily and irresistibly hardened. God used Pharaoh's hard heart to judge him for his past sins and to glorify His Name on the international stage, humiliating Egypt and its gods.

go far from Egypt), saying that it was imperative that Israel obey Yahweh and leave Egypt to serve Him with sacrifice in the wilderness lest Yahweh fall upon them with pestilence and with the sword (i.e., with death). This part of the bargaining was calculated to be less demanding, and it allowed Pharaoh to save face. In granting the request, the (supposedly) divine Pharaoh would not be submitting to the demands of a foreign god, but only taking care of his subject people (and his work force), lest that foreign god take vengeance on his Hebrews for non-compliance.

Pharaoh would have none of it, and he abruptly ended the audience, saying, "Why do you draw the people away from their work quotas? Get back to your brick burdens!" Note that Pharaoh included Moses and Aaron in his demands, regarding them as just another part of the Egyptian labor force.

There was worse to come: in retaliation for such a demand, the Hebrews were ordered to produce the same required number of bricks but were refused the material to make them. Formerly, the Egyptian foremen provided straw as a component for their brickmaking. This straw was now denied them; they would have to find their own straw or stubble, however they could. Obviously, Pharaoh thought, the Hebrews' demand was caused by their laziness. In a word play, the text relates Pharaoh's demand that the Hebrews should work [Hebrew *ya'ashu*], and not listen [Hebrew *yishu*] to lies and nonsense from Moses. More work, less listening to nonsense!

The Hebrews therefore scattered about and scrounged stubble wherever they could find it. The workday was thus spent in foraging, yet the taskmasters still demanded that the full tally of bricks be turned in by day's end. It was an impossible task, and of course resulted only in further beatings when the Hebrews could not provide the bricks. Listening to Moses and Aaron had not brought liberation, but further enslavement. They were worse off than they were before! In anger they turned upon Moses and Aaron after their mission of protest to Pharaoh proved futile and invoked God's judgment on them for making their lives even more miserable than they were before. Moses could not help but feel that he had failed again—as he had warned Yahweh that he would!

After Moses hit rock bottom, Yahweh acted, declaring to Moses that the time of waiting was over: "Now you shall see what I will do to Pharaoh, for by a strong hand [i.e., under compulsion] he will let you go, and by a strong hand he will drive them out of his land" (Exod. 6·1) Yahweh had promised Moses that He was the great I Am, Yahweh, the one with sufficient power to liberate tiny Israel from the mighty superpower of the day and He was about to manifest that power. Over and over again, He repeats "I am Yahweh," the I Am (Exod. 6:2, 6, 7, 8), the One who is able to do whatever He pleased. He had promised to give the land of Canaan to the descendants of Abraham, Isaac, and Jacob, and He was about to keep that promise. Moses conveyed Yahweh's assurance to the sons of Israel, but they were so dispirited from their last experience of Moses' audience with Pharaoh that God's words found no resonance in their hearts. It didn't matter. God was about to act.

The First Contest

The Exodus narrative next records the first contest between Moses and Aaron and the mighty Pharaoh. In this contest, at Moses' direction, Aaron threw down their staff before Pharaoh and it became a tannin.[1] In the initial instructions to Moses, Yahweh said that his staff would become a serpent [Hebrew *nachash*]—i.e., a serpent, or a horrible reptile. In the Sinai, such an animal was a snake, a serpent. In Egypt, such an animal was a *tannin*, possibly a crocodile. At Pharaoh's insistence, his magicians could reproduce the same result with their secret arts.

---

1   The LXX reads a δράκος (*drakon*), a dragon. We note the connection of the crocodile with the Nile in which crocodiles lived.

Yet even so, their arts could not compete with the divine power of Yahweh: though the Egyptians sorcerers threw down their own staffs so that they became *tannin* (possibly crocodiles)[1] which crawled all about, the staff–*tannin* of Moses and Aaron swallowed them up![2] Pharaoh's magicians had power, but the power of Yahweh was greater still. When Moses' staff swallowed up the serpentine staffs of the Egyptian sorcerers, anyone could see that Moses' God would ultimately prove to be the more powerful. But as expected, Pharaoh hardened his heart, and refused to learn the obvious lesson. It was as Yahweh had declared: he would harden Pharaoh's heart, revealing his character before the world, and humiliating him before the nations. The contest between Yahweh and Pharaoh was about to begin in earnest.

— *Lessons from the Lawgiver's Life*

After Moses' disastrous initial audience with Pharaoh he must have felt that he had hit rock bottom. He had left Egypt as a disgraced fugitive years before, and only returned under divine duress because God would not take 'no' for an answer, but insisted that he return and confront Pharaoh with His demand that he let Israel go. Moses had obtained the confidence of the elders of Israel who put their trust in his ability to confront Pharaoh and liberate them from the iron furnace. Despite Moses' courageous and prophetic bearing, Pharaoh categorically refused to listen to him or accept that he spoke not for the Hebrews, but for their God. The more Moses pushed Pharaoh, the more Pharaoh grew adamant, and hostile to him and the Hebrews he represented.

Far from concluding that a deity had indeed spoken to Moses and commissioned him as a messenger, Pharaoh

---

1   Whether through supernatural demonic power, but through sleight-of-hand trickery, we are not told.
2   We note here a touch of humorous mockery at this unexpected turn of events.

concluded that the Israelites were simply lazy and had not enough to do. Why else would they listen to such a wild tale? The solution was plain: give the Hebrews more to do, and punish them for listening to Moses. Behind Pharaoh's assertion that the Hebrews were motivated by their own laziness was the added unspoken political consideration that punishing them for listening to Moses' plan for liberation would serve to deter other groups in Egypt who might contemplate rebellion against Pharaoh. Such independence movements must be nipped in the bud!

Moses obeyed God in throwing down his staff so that it turned into a serpent. But since Pharaoh's magicians and priests could do the same (or at least something like it), Pharaoh was not at all impressed. When Pharaoh decreed that the Hebrews must now make bricks without straw, the people rounded on Moses, invoking divine judgment upon him, and blaming them for their increased misery. Moses' words to Yahweh, "Why did You ever send me?" (Exod. 5:22) was not so much a query as a cry of pain.

None of this came as a surprise to the Lord. He sometimes lets us hit rock bottom so that we might despair of ourselves and cast ourselves more completely upon Him. It is not until we have exhausted every human source of strength that we truly rely upon God. St. Paul discovered this in his own ministry. His ministry in Asia (i.e., Asia Minor) was filled with suffering and persecution. As he wrote to the Corinthians, "In Asia we were burdened excessively, beyond our strength, so that we despaired even of life. Indeed, we had the sentence of death within ourselves so that we would not trust in ourselves, but in God who raises the dead" (2 Cor. 1:8–9). Like St. Paul, we sometimes require a revelation of our own inadequacy and weakness before we really trust God and rely upon His strength.

Day Six
Smiting Egypt: Part I

THE CONTEST BETWEEN YAHWEH and Pharaoh began with Yahweh's declaration to Moses that Pharaoh would only release Israel after a series of "hits," [the Hebrew word used, *nakah*, literally means "to hit"] wherein Yahweh "hit" Egypt with disaster after disaster (customarily referred to as "the ten plagues of Egypt," though the term "plague," which usually notes a medical bacterial pestilence, does not accurately describe the many different disasters with which God struck Egypt). Yahweh had promised Moses that He would smite Egypt with all of His mighty acts (Exod. 3:20), culminating on His final "hit" or smiting of the first born when He would "strike down [Hebrew *nakah*] all the first born in the land of Egypt, both man and beast" (Exod. 12:12). The first "hit" was soon to come.

The First Hit: The Nile Turned to Blood (Exod. 7:14–24)

Moses was instructed to take his symbol of authority, his humble shepherd's staff, and meet Pharaoh as he walked by the bank of the Nile (probably to bathe there). For the Egyptians, the Nile was divine, and had the power to bestow life upon Egypt when it overflowed its banks, giving water to all. But by the power of Yahweh, even the "divine" Nile was overcome so it dealt death, and not life. So, at the command

39

of Yahweh to Moses, Aaron stretched out the staff over the Nile in every direction so as to reach all the various canals, streams, and reservoirs, and "all the water that was in the Nile was turned to blood ... and the blood was throughout all the land of Egypt" (Exod. 7:20–21). It was not just the Nile that was affected, but all the water throughout Egypt. The Hebrew God clearly was sovereign over all of Egypt, and over their gods.

What was meant by blood? The term does not necessarily indicate the fluid that flows through human veins and arteries. The word "blood" [Hebrew dam] was a color as well as a substance (thus the prophet predicted that the moon would be turned to blood—i.e., red in color [Joel 2:31]). In the same way, this word might only mean that all the water of Egypt, both the water flowing down the Nile and the water already collected, would supernaturally become red in color, foul to drink, and deadly to fish. Some commentators suggest that this miracle involved God producing minute fungi and red vegetable matter or tiny insects of reddish hue which rendered the water impossible to drink, supernaturally multiplying such natural disasters as a judgment upon Egypt.[1] Certainly the result was catastrophic: for seven days, the Egyptians could find no water.

Pharaoh, however, once again remained unmoved. His magicians by their secret pagan arts could reproduce this miracle or a reasonable facsimile, with the result that Pharaoh refused to consider that Moses' God was more powerful than the gods of Egypt and should be obeyed. Pharaoh simply turned his back on them all, and walked silently back into his palace, leaving his people to scramble for water as best they could (Exod. 7:23). We note in passing that these

[1]   The comment in Exod. 7:18 that "the Egyptians will be weary in drinking water from the Nile" indicates that the disaster consisted of tainted water, and not actual blood. Had it been actual blood, no one would have attempted to drink it. In v. 21 the liquid is still referred to as "water."

Egyptian sorcerers, though they could reproduce the miracle to Pharaoh's satisfaction, they could not reverse the plague that Yahweh laid upon the land or turn the waters of Egypt back to their original state. Clearly Moses' God had the upper hand.

The Second Hit: Frogs (Exod. 8:1–15)

After the hit upon the water of the Nile came a second hit a mere week later, consisting of Egypt being overwhelmed by frogs, which naturally would leave the Nile if its waters became deadly. Egypt always had an abundance of frogs which swarmed after the retreat of the Nile's annual inundation. After the water receded, the frogs would breed. (Perhaps for this reason frogs were associated with the Egyptian god Hapi and the goddess Heqt who was involved in childbirth.) But this hit far exceeded any natural phenomenon the Egyptians had previously experienced.

The Hebrew word for "frog" is *tsefardea*—an onomatopoeic word which reproduces the croaking sound which frogs make. Thus, Egypt was to be overwhelmed by croakers.

Moses and Aaron did not wait to find Pharaoh outside as previously, but boldly entered the royal palace to find him there and once again present Yahweh's demand that he let His people go. Should Pharaoh again refuse, Egypt would swarm with frogs. This hit would not consist simply of experiencing the frogs which normally left the Nile after it receded. This would be a supernatural infestation: frogs would be everywhere, not simply by the Nile. They would be multiplied until they overwhelmed the nation, from the house of Pharaoh to the houses of his servants. They would enter everyone's home and sleeping quarters, including the mats on which they slept.[1] They would even be found in their ovens (despite the fact that frogs usually avoided dry, warm places to cold, damp places), and in their kneading bowls. So, Moses said to Pharaoh, the frogs would "come up on you"—climbing up the royal legs! Throughout the land people would find the cold, slimy, unsanitary creatures everywhere. There would be no escape: they would sleep with them, eat with them, and be subjected to their ceaseless croaking night and day. If frogs were associated with Hapi and Heqt, this hit reveals Yahweh's sovereignty over these Egyptian deities—He is the one who controls frogs, not the gods of Egypt.

So it happened as Moses threatened. At a divine command from Moses, Aaron stretched out his hand and rod over the rivers, streams, and pools (i.e., turning every direction from where he stood), and frogs indeed began to overwhelm the land. When Pharaoh resorted to his magicians for help, the best they could do was to produce more frogs of their own—though more frogs were hardly helpful!

At last Pharaoh relented and summoned Moses and Aaron, entreating them to ask their God Yahweh to remove the frogs. With ironic courtesy, Moses replied, "The honor is yours to tell me when I shall entreat for you and your servants and our people." Moses would do as Pharaoh asked, leaving him the honor of picking the day. As well as containing a touch of irony in being deferential to someone he was clearly humbling, this detail made it indisputable that the frogs came as a judgment from Yahweh, and not as a simple natural event, for they would die and be left only in the Nile on the exact day that Pharaoh chose. Not surprisingly, Pharaoh chose the earliest time possible: "tomorrow."

And so it was; on the very next day all the frogs died, and were left only in the Nile where they belonged. The fact that

---

[1]   The ancient Egyptians did not sleep on elevated beds as those in developed countries do, but on mats on the floor—quite accessible to frogs.

the dead frogs were piled in such great heaps that the land stank was a silent monument to Yahweh's power. And yet Pharaoh's heart remained silent, as well.

The Third Hit: Biting Insects (Exod. 8:16–19)

The third blow upon Egypt began after the divine command came to Aaron telling him to stretch out his staff and hit the dust of the earth. This act of hitting the earth would loosen and scatter the grains of topsoil, an image of how tiny biting insects would be scattered throughout the land. The Hebrew word here rendered a "biting insect" is *kinnim*. The ancients did not differentiate species of animals with the same precision that we moderns do. (For example, the Greek ἀετόςae-tos may refer to either a vulture or an eagle). Here the word *kinnim* might refer to gnats or mosquitoes, and most likely refers to a swarm of many such flying, biting insects. They swarmed throughout the land, as common as the dust of the earth, afflicting men and animals, causing painful skin irritation, especially since they could creep into the nose and eyes.

When Pharaoh appealed to his staff magicians, they could not produce anything like this. They could only report to Pharaoh their helplessness, admitting that this was not some trickery or magic from Moses and Aaron, but "the finger of God" (Exod. 8:19). This phrase refers to truly divine activity, direct from God Himself (compare the use of the phrase in Exod. 31:18). Despite this admission on the part of his staff magicians with their implied counsel of submission to the God who did this, Pharaoh's heart remained hardened.

Day Seven
Smiting Egypt: Part II

The Fourth Hit: A Mixture of Flying Insects (Exod. 8:20–32)

MOSES THEN WENT TO PHARAOH as he went for his (possibly daily) bath in the Nile and presented him once more with Yahweh's demand that he let His people go to serve Him. Refusal would result in a mixture of flying insects being let loose upon him, his servants, and all his people, to be found throughout their homes, and upon all the ground beneath their feet. They wouldn't even be able to put a foot on the ground without stepping on them! But here a detail is added for the first time: this disaster would not touch the Hebrews who lived in the land of Goshen (i.e., the eastern Nile delta of Egypt). This part of Egypt would remain untouched, revealing that the swarm was not a natural disaster befalling Egypt by chance, but a divine judgment on Pharaoh's stubbornness.

The word here translated "mixture" is Hebrew *arob*. Its meaning is less than clear, so that a Targum[1] paraphrase of the text renders it as "wild animals" (which is surely incor-

---

1   Targum was an Aramaic paraphrase of the Hebrew Torah, of a type made from about the first century A.D. when Hebrew was declining as a spoken language.

rect). It seems to refer here to a mixed swarm, a cloud huge enough to contain many different flying insects, some of which would bite. The Septuagint translators, who lived in Egypt, rendered the word as κυνόμυια (*kunomui*), "a dog fly," which sucked blood from those it bit, causing eye disease and blindness. Perhaps that is why Psalm 78:45 speaks of the swarm as "devouring" the Egyptians. If the *kinnim* ("biting insects") of the previous hit were characterized by their tiny size which allowed them to creep into any orifice, this *arob* referred to a mixed swarm of immense size—a cloud of flying, biting insects.

The mixed swarm, promised by Moses for the next day, came right on time, laying waste the whole land—except for Goshen where the Hebrews dwelt unharmed. After so many disasters, Pharaoh now summoned Moses and Aaron to offer a compromise (after a lapse of how many days we are not told—enough to ruin life in Egypt; v. 24). He was now prepared to bargain with Yahweh in a way that he hadn't been willing before. Their God wanted them to sacrifice to Him, and Pharaoh would allow them to do that—but only if they stayed and served Him thus within the land of Egypt. The demand to go and sacrifice in the wilderness after a journey of three days (i.e., a journey from which they would not return) was still out of the question.

Moses does not simply disallow the counteroffer but gives a reason why it was impractical: "It is not right to do so, for we will sacrifice to Yahweh our God what is an abomination to the Egyptians." Moses thus responded according the conventions of his day, acting as if Pharaoh's counteroffer was acceptable in principle, but still flawed—the flaw being that the Egyptians found the Hebrews' sacrifices of sheep abominable (see Gen. 46:34), and would stone the Hebrews if they saw them offering these sacrifices in their midst. In fact, Pharaoh's counteroffer was completely unacceptable, for what Yahweh demanded from the outset, under the diplomatic guise of a three day migration from Egypt, was the complete and permanent exodus of His people from Egypt—and both Pharaoh and Moses knew this. Pharaoh was again refusing the initial demand and trying to substitute something else: a brief holiday from work, followed by a return to perpetual Egyptian servitude.

Upon hearing Moses' response, Pharaoh capitulated, allowing Israel to leave the country for their sacrifice—only further requesting that they not go very far (i.e., that they soon return). He would do anything—just ask Yahweh to remove the swarm from Egypt! Moses accepted the capitulation, warning Pharaoh not to renege on the agreement (warning him politely, in the third person: "let not Pharaoh deal falsely again"). Moses then departed to intercede for Pharaoh and ask God that the mixed swarm be removed. God hearkened to Moses and removed the swarm, only to have Moses find that Pharaoh of course hardened his heart after obtaining relief.

The Fifth Hit: Pestilence on the Cattle (Exod. 9:1–7)

The next disaster to befall Egypt was announced with the by-now customary demand that Pharaoh submit to Yahweh's demand to let His people go that they might serve Him, far from their Egyptian servitude. Once again Moses and Aaron walked into Pharaoh's palace to confront him personally. Refusal to submit to their demand would result in a pestilence which would come straight from the hand of God—i.e., a mighty pestilence indeed. It would fall upon all their domestic animals—the livestock in their fields, their horses (used for warfare), their donkeys and camels (used for transport), and on their herds and flocks. Together these animals constituted the wealth of an agrarian community like Egypt, and widespread death among these animals would be an economic catastrophe of immense proportions. Moreover, the Hebrews' exemption from this catastrophe could constitute a national humiliation as well—for Pharaoh, his people, and their gods.

And that exemption for Israel is precisely what Yahweh promised: a pestilence [Hebrew *deber*] would fall upon Egyptians' cattle, but to the Hebrews' cattle nothing [Hebrew *lo dabar*] would happen.[1] To further confirm that this pestilence was no mere natural occurrence, but came from the hand of Yahweh, Moses set the date for its onset: tomorrow (v. 5).

It turned out exactly as foretold. The next day all the cattle of the Egyptians were afflicted and many died, but none of the Hebrews' livestock were affected. To make sure that what Moses said about the Hebrews' exemption from the plague had come true, Pharaoh sent men to investigate the situation. And sure enough, "of the livestock of the sons of Israel, not one died" (Exod. 9:6). The purpose of the investigation was to determine if this was so, for if it were true, it proved conclusively the divine and supernatural nature of the plague. Yet even after Pharaoh learned from those he sent that it was so, he still hardened his heart and refused Yahweh's demand. The king's stubbornness was fast becoming perverse and irrational—and increasingly culpable.

The Sixth Hit: Pustules (Exod. 9:8–12)

The next audience of Moses and Aaron with Pharaoh took place outdoors. This time they took with them a container that held ashen soot which they had gathered from their full cupped hands[2] from a furnace kiln. As instructed by Yahweh, in the sight of Pharaoh they took cupped handfuls of the black ash and cast it into the sky where the wind would carry it away. By the power of Yahweh the soot would "become dust over all the land of Egypt, and will become pustules breaking out with sores on man and beast throughout

---

1   We note the play on words: *lo dabar* also means "pastureless."

2   The usual rendering "handfuls" is too constrained and allows for not enough soot. The Hebrew reads, "the fullness of your cupped hands."

all the land of Egypt." The word rendered here "pustules" is often rendered "boils," but it signifies not what we normally regard as simple boils, but as festering, putrefying sores and skin ulcers. Deut. 28:27 refers to the pustules of Egypt, mentioning also tumors and itchy scabs. Some have suggested that the pustules were the symptoms of skin anthrax, which caused black, burning abscesses—reminiscent of the soot thrown from the furnace. Whatever the exact diagnosis, the affliction was loathsome and painful.

Why did Yahweh command them to use soot from a furnace as the catalyst for divine action? Possibly because the soot from the furnace provided an image of the hot and sweaty toil of the Hebrews, who labored in Egypt as in an iron furnace (Deut. 4:20). The black soot of their slavery caused the Egyptians to suffer in retaliation, as both man and beast suffered from this affliction. The magicians, who were to have functioned as physicians who alleviated pain, were also afflicted, and so could provide no help at all. For all their vaunted Egyptian secret arts, they could not save themselves from the judgment of Yahweh.

Day Eight
Smiting Egypt: Part III

The Seventh Hit: Hail (Exod. 9:13–35)

THE CALAMITY OF THE HAIL is narrated in great detail—twenty-three verses in all, compared to a mere eight verses for the sign of the pestilence on the cattle and five verses for the sign of the pustules. With the beginning of this third round of three judgments upon Egypt, it appeared that Yahweh's patience began to wear thin, and the challenges to Pharaoh's stubborn pride and obstinacy became ever more pronounced. An element of prophetic denunciation was added to Moses' confrontations with Pharaoh, and the signs of judgment upon Egypt accordingly grew ever more severe and fierce.

Accordingly, Moses' message to Pharaoh after he found him in the early morning contained not just another demand for Israel's release, but a declaration of Yahweh's power. Up until now Yahweh had been holding back. Pharaoh was still standing not because Yahweh could not overthrow him, but because Yahweh had been patient; Pharaoh's survival was not a testimony to Pharaoh's strength, but to Yahweh's restraint. But the time for such restraint had passed. "This time," Yahweh declared, "I will send all My plagues to your heart and to your servants and your people." If Yahweh had put forth

His hand and hit [Hebrew *nakah*] them all with pestilence without restraint, Pharaoh would have been cut off from the earth. The only reason Pharaoh was still standing was so that Yahweh could proclaim His name (i.e., His power) through all the earth by humbling Pharaoh on the world stage.

After this prophetic denunciation of Pharaoh's sinful pride in refusing to let Yahweh's people go came the announcement of the next hit: "Behold! About this time tomorrow, I will send a very heavy hail, such as has not been seen in Egypt from the day it was founded until now." Heavy hailstorms were rare in Egypt, especially compared to Palestine, so this sign would be the more impressive. Hailstorms in particular seem to have been regarded as signs of heavenly wrath. In Joshua 10:11, Yahweh threw large stones upon Israel's enemies as they fled, killing many of them. In Revelation 16:21ff hailstones came as the culmination of all God's outpoured wrath upon Babylon, the climax of a series of ever-escalating judgments. Hail was not simply a meteorological event for the ancients; it was an image of divine wrath.

The announcement of the time when the hail would come also served to test the Egyptians—those who had seen Yahweh's power and had come to believe in the might of the Hebrews' deity could take warning, and protect themselves from the coming onslaught, while those who disbelieved would ignore the warning, and would leave themselves and their animals in the unprotected outdoors. Yahweh Himself showed His compassion in telling Pharaoh to give this fair warning to his people, so that those Egyptians who so wished could save themselves.[1] The hail was to destroy their crops, but any who foolishly ignored the warning given by the He-

---

1   This was necessary because cattle were not usually housed in stables in Egypt as they are in northern Europe but were left outside—especially during this season of January–April when the hailstorm occurred. Horses might be stabled, but not livestock. Those wishing to save their livestock must therefore bring the animals into their homes, or find room in their grain storage sheds.

brews' God would suffer further damage and even loss of life.

At Moses' signal, Yahweh sent thunder, lightning ("fire"), and hail upon the earth. It struck down all the crops growing in the field, bringing the promise of hunger to those whose crops were ruined,[1] as well as inflicting injury and even death upon those left unprotected outside. But, as before, the land of Goshen where the Hebrews lived remained untouched and serene.

This time, Pharaoh relented, acknowledging that he had done wrong by Israel's deity. But his declaration, "I have sinned this time; Yahweh is the righteous one, and I and my people are the wicked ones" should not be construed as an expression of heartfelt contrition, but simply as an admission that Yahweh's rights as a deity were legitimate and that Pharaoh had done wrong in not granting them. Pharaoh was not consumed with guilt, as one trained in Christian spirituality might imagine. He was entering a plea of "guilty as charged" in court and admitting he had been in the wrong. On this basis he asked Moses to intercede and ask his deity to make the hailstorm cease.

As soon as Moses returned to his people, he made the requested intercession, and God responded by ending the storm, so that it was no longer even raining. But when the sky cleared, Pharaoh immediately hardened his heart yet again. This was not unexpected, and lest one should imagine that Moses had been duped, the narrator records that before Moses left Pharaoh's presence he said as a parting shot, "As for you and your servants, I know that you do not yet fear

---

1   A note in Exod. 9:31–32 records that it was the flax and barley that were hit [Hebrew *nakah*], not the wheat and spelt which came up later. This explains why there was still food for the coming locusts to devour later on. It also helps date the hit: it came no later than January, for the flax and barley were harvested in February–March. The wheat and spelt were harvested in March–April. The note also shows that the hits came not one right after another, but weeks and months apart, possibly from late autumn or winter to early spring.

before Yahweh Elohim,"[1] the Hebrews' God. The use of the compound divine name (as used in Gen. 2:4; 3:1, 23) is unusual. Its use here indicates the full majesty of the God of Israel: He is Yahweh, the God of the Hebrews, as well as Elohim, the God over all the earth. Pharaoh was treating Him with insufficient reverence, as if He were just another deity whose claims for cultic service must be granted.

The Eighth Hit: Locusts (Exod. 10:1–20)

The sacred text also relates this hit at length, and begins with Yahweh saying to Moses that this contest is being prolonged, not because He does not possess power to overwhelm Egypt immediately, but because He is making a laughingstock of the mighty Egyptians by hardening Pharaoh's heart so that Pharaoh continually refuses the obvious course of action to release the Hebrews. This unprecedented victory over the superpower of the day whereby Yahweh made fools of them all would be repeated father to son throughout the generations. This victory revealed, unequivocally, that Yahweh was God, the God who did whatever He willed.

After this Moses and Aaron went to Pharaoh in his palace, and began the audience by sternly rebuking Pharaoh for his prideful stubbornness: "How long," they asked with prophetic denunciation, "will you refuse to humble yourself before Me?" Continued refusal to submit would result tomorrow in Yahweh bringing locusts throughout Egypt, locusts which would darken the whole surface of the ground and eat everything that the hailstorm left and fill up their homes. After delivering this fearful ultimatum, Moses and Aaron turned on their heels and left, without waiting for an answer. They had come as prophetic messengers of doom, not as diplomatic negotiators.

As soon as Moses and Aaron left, Pharaoh's servants spoke to him with great boldness: "How long will this man

---

1   Usually translated, "The Lord God."

be a snare to us? Let the men go, that they may serve Yahweh their god. Do you not know that Egypt is ruined?" Usually Pharaoh's servants would never have dared to speak so plainly, but the situation was desperate. Pestilence had destroyed much of their livestock, and the hailstorms had further destroyed the remaining livestock and crops. A swarm of locusts eating everything that remained would finish Egypt, bringing famine upon the land, and death for much of the population. In this situation, they felt that they had no choice but to speak to Pharaoh with such daring.

Their strategy succeeded, and Moses and Aaron were hurriedly brought back to Pharaoh. Pharaoh began the audience by capitulating to their demands: "Go and serve Yahweh your god!" But he then pulled back, and asked, "Who are the ones who will be going?" thereby resuming the process of negotiation. When Moses said, "We shall go with our young and our old, with our sons and our daughters, with our flocks and our herds" (not asking Pharaoh, but telling him), Pharaoh balked, and spoke with heated irony, "May Yahweh indeed be with you if ever I let you and your little ones go!" He would allow the men [Hebrew *geber*, the young men] to go, but not their women, children, or flocks, since that was what Moses demanded. With that, Pharaoh drove them from his presence before they could reply. It was, of course, yet another instance of Pharaoh resisting and refusing the demand of Yahweh. Accordingly, Moses responded with judgment.

Moses stretched forth his hand over the land, and Yahweh brought an east wind all that day and night, bringing a swarm of locusts upon the land of Egypt. By the following morning, locusts began settling over all of Egypt, covering the land and eating every plant in sight. A famine threatened the very life of Egypt, given the previous disasters, and Pharaoh therefore summoned Moses and Aaron, offering again his capitulation, and in the most abject way, asking for forgiveness for the sin of refusing the just demands of a god: "Please forgive my sin only this once, and make supplication for me to Yahweh your god, that He may remove this death from me"—death indeed, for if the locust infestation continued, famine would kill off most of the people. Moses left Pharaoh's presence to again pray to Yahweh to spare Egypt. Yahweh did, sending a wind to drive the locust swarm eastward into the Red Sea. Yet, as one by now might expect, Pharaoh hardened his heart after relief came, and reneged on his promise of liberation.

The Ninth Hit: Darkness (Exod. 10:21–29)

The last of the three cycles of hits followed immediately after the eighth. Yahweh said to Moses, "Stretch out your hand toward the sky, that there may be darkness over the land of Egypt, even a darkness which may be felt." Moderns reading this must leave their technological world of artificial lighting, light bulbs, and night lights and try to realize the horror which ancient people had of the dark. To be deprived of light was the ultimate horror (see Matt. 8:12; 22:13; 25:30; Jude 6, 13), and so total darkness was a terror to be avoided at all costs. Nighttime was a time of vulnerability, a time when one stayed inside, waiting for the rising of the sun, the opening of the city gates, and the return of life. Night was the time of death. In Egypt, bringing darkness on the land was perceived as an assault on the Egyptian sungod, whose beneficence and victory over the darkness the Egyptians praised every morning.

The darkness which Moses brought upon Egypt was a darkness which could be felt—i.e., a darkness so dark that one would have to grope and feel one's way to move. It lasted three days, during which no one affected could move or leave their home or resume life. Most commentators suggest that this darkness was caused by a *khamsin*, a sandstorm which indeed could be felt and cause one to grope and feel one's way. They were not unknown in Egypt, and here one of tremendous force served the purposes of Yahweh to judge Egypt—

as was clear from the fact that it did not affect the Hebrews in Goshen. This was no ordinary *khamsin*!

Once again Pharaoh summoned Moses and relented. Yet even now he tried vainly to negotiate: the Hebrew men could leave along with their women and children, but they must leave their flocks behind, in token that they would return. This was of course yet another refusal of Yahweh's demand that His people leave Egypt, and Moses of course refused this condition. Continuing with the convention of bargaining and negotiating, Moses insisted that the flocks accompany Israel because the Hebrews would not know until they arrived at their destination what Yahweh might ask them to sacrifice.

Moses was emphatic that no compromise was possible: "Not a hoof shall be left behind." Pharaoh would have none of it and knew that Moses was diplomatically refusing his compromise. He therefore angrily responded, "Get away from me! Beware! You shall not see my face again, for in the day you see my face, you shall die!" Thus did Pharaoh draw his line in the Egyptian sand. There would be no more compromises or negotiations: Pharaoh had experienced enough of Moses' games and the unreasonable demands of this foreign god. The next time Moses approached Pharaoh with another demand or threat, he would have him killed. Moses had seen enough also: "You are right—you shall never see my face again!" It was over. No more negotiations, no more demands. But Israel was still in slavery and still required to make bricks or be beaten when the unreasonable demands were not met. What would happen next?

— *Lessons from the Lawgiver's Life*

Pharaoh's repeated attempts to deny God's demands or negotiate with Him were what led Egypt to catastrophe. Submission to God at the beginning would have saved tremendous suffering and loss of life, but Pharaoh thought that it would be better to deny God's demands for total obedience and imagined that somehow such refusal to submit would produce happiness. We might blame Pharaoh for his perversity and hardness of heart, but in much of our life we imitate the king of Egypt in refusing to obey God.

That is because our refusal to submit to God is not couched in terms of refusal, but of silent and unacknowledged negotiation. We believe, for example, that all of our time is our own, and we decide for ourselves how much of it we will give to God—bargaining a Sunday morning in exchange for a religious "checkmark" of good standing. We might believe that all our wealth is our own, and decide for ourselves how much of that we will give to God—perhaps a small contribution to a charity every Christmas time. Because God is God and because our happiness depends upon our constant communion with Him, God demands all—all that we are we must give to Him. Like Pharaoh, we think we can negotiate, and give God some portion of our life, but not all.

In this we fail to see that there is no such thing as partial obedience. Because God demands all of our heart and all of our life, we can either give Him what He demands, or refuse it. We can either obey or disobey. But negotiation is not possible, and what we might think is partial obedience is simply disobedience. God does not negotiate, nor make treaties accepting our partial obedience, because only our complete obedience will secure our eternal happiness.

C. S. Lewis discovered this at the beginning of his journey of faith. In his memoir Surprised by Joy, he wrote of his final submission to God in these words:

> What had been an ideal became a command; and what might not be expected of one? Doubtless, by definition, God was Reason itself. But would He also be "reasonable" in that other, more comfortable, sense? Not the slightest assurance on that score was offered me. Total surrender, the absolute leap in the

dark, were demanded. The reality with which no treaty can be made was upon me. The demand was not even "All or nothing." Now, the demand was simply "All."[1]

Pharaoh discovered that meeting God was an encounter with the reality with which no treaty could be made. What God demanded of Pharaoh, He demands of everyone, for He desires that everyone be saved. There is no negotiating; the demand is simply "All."

1   C. S. Lewis, *Surprised by Joy* (Glasgow: Collins Fount Paperbacks, 1982), p. 182.

Day Nine
The Passover

Announcing the Tenth Hit: The Death of the First born

THE LONG-PROMISED MOMENT of liberation was at hand, and the sign of this was Moses' direction to Israel to ask for gifts of silver and gold from their Egyptian overlords,[1] for this request would not have been made if the time of their departure were not near. By now the Egyptians were more than happy to give such gifts to the Hebrews. The reason stated is that "Yahweh gave them favor in the sight of the Egyptians"—in other words, the events of the last weeks and months had convinced the Egyptians that the god of the Hebrews who worked through Moses was mighty indeed, and so the Hebrews' request for gifts should be granted. This granting of gifts was thus one more sign of Yahweh's might, for the gifts the Egyptians gave to the Hebrews was the Egyptian acknowledgment of the power of the Hebrew God over Egypt.

Yahweh revealed to Moses that He was about to go forth

---

[1] The word "neighbor," often used here in English translations, should not be read so as to give the impression that the Egyptians and Hebrews lived side by side, or next door to each other. The Hebrews lived in Goshen, apart from the Egyptians for whom they worked.

throughout Egypt at midnight, when the Egyptians were asleep and defenseless, and all the first born [Hebrew *bekor*, the best of them] would be struck down, from the first born of Pharaoh on his high throne to the first born of the humblest, the female slave who labored grinding the family's daily bread early in the morning by the millstones. Rank, age, and gender counted for nothing: the best and first born of every Egyptian, man, woman, high, low, human or beast, would be struck down by God. But this blow which affected absolutely everyone in Egypt would not touch the Hebrews in the eastern part of Egypt. Nothing would trouble their peace—not even a dog would growl against them. This was a sign that this disaster came from Yahweh, the God of the Hebrews, and not from random chance.

Moses gave this message to Pharaoh, in defiance of Pharaoh's refusal to admit him to his presence under penalty of death, and then stormed out from Pharaoh's presence in hot anger. Moses' anger at Pharaoh's continual breaking of his promises to release Israel mirrored God's own impatience; there would be no more such audiences with the king of Egypt, or warning messages from the Israel's God.

Moses therefore turned from Pharaoh to Israel, from the frustrating past to the glorious future. We see this in the texts which follow, for they concern not only the Hebrews' contemporary experience as they left Egypt, but also include provisions for their future life in the Promised Land. Liberation from Egyptian slavery was now so certain and so imminent that instructions could be given for life after Egypt.[1] The instructions in Exod. 12 regarding how Israel should keep the Passover feast after they had left Egypt were thus no interruption of the narrative flow, but the fruit of it. The

---

[1] Thus Exod. 12:1 stresses the fact that the instructions for keeping the Passover in perpetuity were given "in Egypt." The geographical marker also reveals that some of the instructions which followed (e.g., v. 11) were only intended for that first Passover night.

terror of Passover night in Egypt would lead to a life of peace in the Promised Land—where such instructions regarding annually commemorating the Passover deliverance would be needed.

Preparing for the Passover Night

Yahweh turned Moses' attention to the future by declaring that "This month shall be the beginning of months for you; it is to be the first month of the year to you" (Exod. 12:2). Their calendar in Egypt (as in many cultures) used to begin in the autumn; now it would begin in the spring, at the time when Yahweh set them free. As well as serving to form another cultural difference between Israel and the Canaanites in the Promised Land, a calendar which began in the spring served to anchor the daily life of the Israelites in the mighty acts of God. The counting of calendar months would serve to remind them that they only possessed the Promised Land on which they lived and farmed because Yahweh had freed them from Egyptian slavery.

The instructions contain a mixture of directives unique to Passover night and those which pertained to the Passover celebrations in the succeeding years. A few days before the fourteenth day of that month they must take a small kid from the flock for themselves, either a lamb or a goat (the Hebrew word *seh* could refer to either), a male about a year old,[1] and without physical blemish (such as lameness or blindness), since it was to be used in the service of Yahweh. It was to be slaughtered at twilight, when there was still enough light to prepare the animal.

The animal was to be eaten in the traditional way, inherited from Israel's nomadic forefathers—i.e., not boiled, but

---

1   Usually only the male animals were eaten; the females were saved for breeding and milking. Since lambing took place in the spring, these animals were about a year old by the time of the Passover.

roasted over a spit after being skinned. It was to be eaten with bitter herbs as a side dish, such as wild lettuce, and unleavened bread—all ancient practices, connecting Israel with their nomadic forefathers. It must be eaten entirely, with none left over until morning for breakfast, and to accomplish this families were allowed to join together according to family size and individual appetite. Eating it on the fourteenth day of the month ensured that the meal would take place under a full moon. On that first Passover night, the meal was to be eaten fully dressed, with everyone ready for a quick departure: they must eat it with loins girded (i.e., cloaks tucked into belts, as one did when traveling), with their sandals on, and with their staff in their hands (despite the fact that sandals were usually not worn, nor staffs carried indoors, since staffs were for protection and herding outside).

The Passover night was indeed unique—a night of anxious vigil for Israel and a night of terror for Egypt. The Israelites were to take some of the blood of the lamb or goat they had slaughtered and daub it with hyssop on the doorposts and lintels of their dwellings. This would serve as a sign that the family within had obeyed Yahweh. As faithful Israelites, they had kept Yahweh's Passover so that the destroyer who passed through Egypt that night with Yahweh to strike down the firstborn would not strike down their firstborn. Thus, Yahweh would "pass over" them and not destroy them (Exod. 12:11–13). The liturgical term "Yahweh's Passover" is here connected with the verb "to pass over" [Hebrew *pasach*], which can also mean "to skip, to limp."[1] The idea is that when Yahweh's destroyer sees the blood he will "skip over" that dwelling and pass on to the next one.

The annual feast of Yahweh's Passover would commemorate this night of fear and deliverance ever after, uniting Israel

---

1   Thus 1 Kings 18:26 uses this verb of the priests of Baal who "skip" about their altar, and 1 Kings 18:21 uses the verb to describe Israel who "limp" between two opinions.

to Yahweh in bonds of faithfulness and gratitude. Each year they were to reenact this slaughter of the lambs or goats and eat them with unleavened bread and bitter herbs. The original Passover meal in Egypt preserved some elements of the traditional diet of their nomadic forefathers such as eating meat roasted and not boiled, and using unleavened bread and simple herbs, such as wild lettuce. Now some of these elements would serve the additional purpose of reminding Israel of the night of their deliverance: the unleavened bread would now remind them of the haste accompanying the first Passover meal when there was no time for the bread to rise, and the bitter herbs would now remind them of their bitter slavery in Egypt. It would serve as a perpetual liturgical reminder of God's deliverance, spread over seven days. Beginning with Passover night, the Israelites would eat unleavened bread for seven days. It would seem that the expansion of the original Passover meal into a feast lasting seven days was intended to transform what might have been regarded as a simple meal into a feast of national unity, binding Israel to their Lord.

The Tenth Hit: The Death of the Firstborn

In the middle of the night, Yahweh hit [Hebrew *nakah*] all the firstborn in the land of Egypt, missing no family, from the throne down to the dungeon, including all the firstborn of cattle.[1] Pharaoh rose up in the night to discover what every other Egyptian had discovered—that death had touched everyone, so that a great cry[2] went up from Egypt. Pharaoh summoned Moses and Aaron in haste and told them, "Get out from among my people, both you and the sons of Israel!

---

1   This detail witnesses to the close connection between man and animal in the family unit in the ancient agricultural world.
2   The same Hebrew word used to describe the cry of the Hebrews under the Egyptian lash in Exod. 3:7.

Worship Yahweh as you have said. Take both your flocks and your herds as you have said and go." Note that Pharaoh no longer described them as "Hebrews" (a term of contempt), but as "the sons of Israel." Note too the repetition of "as you have said": now there is total capitulation, with no conditions. Now they may do as they wanted. We note also a final ironic and bitter parting shot: "and bless me also as you go!"—you whose presence has been such a curse to us!

The news was greeted in Israel with joy. As they left, they asked their Egyptian counterparts for gifts, as they had been directed. The Egyptians, still reeling from the deaths of their loved ones scant hours before, were only too happy to see Israel go. Their continued presence among them could only bring more death. Thus, the narrative comments, Israel "plundered the Egyptians," regarding these gifts as spoils of war. Indeed, Israel was now not a ghetto of slaves, but a victorious army[1] on the march.[2]

As the hosts of Yahweh left Egypt, the narrator mentions that Moses took with him the bones (i.e., the mummy) of Joseph, since before he died Joseph made his brothers swear that they would exhume his body and rebury him in the Promised Land when God finally brought Israel there. The detail is significant, for it reveals how completely Israel's

---

1 Thus, Israel is described as Yahweh's *tsebaʾoth*, hosts, military divisions in Exod. 6:26; 12:41, 51.

2 The size of this army has been much debated. Some suggest that the figure of adult men cited in Exod. 12:37 is too large, given that it would involve a total Hebrew population of over two million—far too large to fit into the land of Goshen, and dwarfing the size of other armies of that day. It is also inconsistent with Exod. 23:29–30, which describes Israel as too small to take over the Promised Land right away, though with a population of over two million they could certainly have instantly overwhelmed the Canaanites in the Promised Land. Scholars point to the fact that the word often rendered "thousand" [Hebrew *ʾeleph*] is also translated "companies or families" in such places as Josh. 22:21, so that the text perhaps should be read as "six hundred families [or clans]."

connection with Egypt had been severed. Joseph during his lifetime rose to position of power and rank in Egypt as Pharaoh's vizier. He had an Egyptian name and an Egyptian wife, the daughter of an Egyptian priest. In appearance and lifestyle, he was thoroughly Egyptian—as one might expect from the vizier—so much so that even his own brothers did not recognize him at first. When he died, he was mummified and placed in a coffin in Egypt. Yet he never forgot the promise of his God, that He would bring Israel into the Promised Land, and Joseph's desire to be reburied in Palestine revealed that though he was in the Egyptian world, he was not truly of the Egyptian world. With his postmortem departure from Egypt, the Hebrews' last link with the place of their sojourn and slavery was broken. Even so thoroughly an Egyptian as Joseph had left that land. He was a symbol for all the people of Israel who were finally shedding their Egyptian past.

— *Lessons from the Lawgiver's Life*

Those who retreated past the doorposts and lintels into the safety of their Hebrew homes in Egypt during that night of Passover terror left some lessons for us who remember that night of fear and freedom.

The first is that the place of eternal safety is within the covenant people of God, those to whom God has spoken His word—that is, within the Church of Christ. The angel of death strikes those who choose to remain outside this saving fold. Entering the Church means crossing a border, leaving a land of danger and death and coming to a refuge and a haven, finding security in a place where Satan and death cannot enter.

That means that apostasy from the Church, or expulsion from it, involves returning to the land where Satan oppresses and where death rules. We see this from the words of St. Paul: the offender who was expelled from the Church for grievous and stubborn sin was "handed over to Satan" (1 Cor. 5:5).

The whole world lies in the power of the Evil One, who rules this age as its god (1 John 5:19; 2 Cor. 4:4). Those entering into the Church through baptism escape his power and defy his rule, turning from darkness to light, and from the dominion of Satan to that of God (Acts 26:18).

But we only remain free of Satan's dominion when we remain in the Church, walking through the world as the disciples of Jesus. Renouncing our faith and our Lord and leaving the Church returns us to the devil's dominion. Departure from the Church—either voluntarily through apostasy or forcibly through excommunication—means abandoning the safety our Hebrew home with the blood over the doorpost and lintels and returning to Egypt. In Egypt, the destroyer will strike us down.

The second lesson we may learn from that Passover night is that our freedom and safety come as the result of shed blood. The New Testament writers are unanimous that the cleansing of the cosmos and the healing of our souls comes as a result of the violent death and shed blood of Jesus (Rom. 5:9; Col. 1:20; Heb. 9:13–14; 1 Pet. 1:19; 1 John 1:7; Rev. 1:5). Christianity is not simply yet another system of ethical exhortations, and Christ did not come merely to offer a moral example. His death was not an unforeseen tragic martyrdom: it was a voluntary self-offering, a deliberate sacrifice which takes away the sin of the world.

In Christ's sacrificial offering, a historical progression, traceable through the succeeding calendars of the people of God. Originally Israel, like all other agricultural people, had an agricultural calendar, marking the times of birth, growth, and harvest. In spring the lambs were born, and in the spring one would slaughter a lamb to feast upon it. Then, at Passover night in the time of Moses, a historical element was added to this agricultural calendar, and the slaughter of the lambs in the spring was then taken up to commemorate annually the slaughter of the Passover lambs in Egypt, reminding Israel of their deliverance from Egypt and their rebirth as a nation.

Now, in the Church, a final Christological element has been added: now Passover[1] commemorates the slaughter of Christ, the true and saving Lamb of God who sacrificed Himself for us at Passover time.

A new layer of meaning was added with the succession of years, as God acted to lead and save His people. First a historical layer was added, transforming a mere agricultural event (the slaughter of the lambs in spring) into a historical commemoration of God's saving act in Egypt. Then a further Christological layer was added, commemorating God's saving act in Christ. Throughout, we see the significance of the death and the blood of the lamb, slowly revealed in the history of the Hebrew people.

---

[1]   In Hebrew *pesach*; in Greek *pascha*.

Day Ten
Salvation at the Red Sea

ISRAEL'S ROUTE AFTER LEAVING Egypt did not take them straight into the Promised Land, for that would have taken them through the land of the Philistines, which was heavily garrisoned—and they were not heading to Palestine directly, but to Mount Sinai. Furthermore, they were not ready for the military confrontation that would have ensued, since as a nation of slaves they had no experience of discipline or even how to handle weapons. Rather they went by the way of the wilderness to the Red Sea.[1] God led them, guiding them from the pillar which went before them, showing them the way. By day it was a pillar of cloud, and by night, a pillar of fire, so that they might travel even after sundown.

The route out of Egypt was particularly circuitous; they traveled southeast, and then doubled back northward, giving the watching Egyptians the impression that they were lost—and vulnerable. It was the last of Yahweh's strategy to humiliate the might of Egypt. When Pharaoh saw that Israel was apparently lost, he hardened his heart yet again, and decided to recapture the work force which he had released a few

---

1   In Hebrew, *Yam Suph*, literally "the Sea of Reeds," probably one the Ballah Lakes. For the sake of familiarly, we continue to use here the traditional name "the Red Sea."

days ago. Taking the best chariots of Egypt, he pursued Israel with a force of six hundred chariots and horsemen. When Israel saw the might of Egypt thundering after them, they panicked and rounded on Moses, whom they had just before hailed as their deliverer.

"Is it because there are no graves in Egypt that you brought us out to die in the wilderness?" They now remembered how they had rejected his leadership when he first returned to Egypt from Midian, and how they concluded that his was a mad plan. They were right in the first place and should never have listened to Moses! Servitude in Egypt was better than death far from home! Even apart from their lack of faith, their repudiation of Moses was wrong: the Egyptians were not coming to kill them, but to reclaim them and return them to the labor of building.

Moses was unmoved, trusting in Yahweh. "Do not fear!" he called out. "Take your stand and see Yahweh's salvation! Yahweh will fight for you while you keep silent!" The people of Israel saw only doom: Egyptian chariots bearing down upon them while they could not go forward to escape because they had reached the sea. But the word came from Yahweh: "Go forward!"—i.e., pack up and prepare to advance. The divine pillar of cloud, the angel of Yahweh,[1] then moved from before Israel to a place behind them, blocking the Egyptian advance. Meanwhile, at God's command, Moses stretched out his staff over the sea and an east wind began to blow. All night long it blew, pushing back the water of the sea, and revealing dry land. The Egyptians could do nothing, for the pillar of fire stood between them and their prey.

The phenomenon of the wind drying up the waters of this region was not unknown. But this occurrence was supernat-

---

1   The pillar is referred to here as "the angel of Yahweh" because it moved from place to place. See footnote on the reference to the "angel of Yahweh" in Exod. 3:2 above in chapter 4 on the Burning Bush.

urally used by God to deliver Israel, both in the extent of the drying water and its timing. The miracle took all night to accomplish (Exod. 14:21), but when it was done the waters formed a barrier (poetically "a wall") on either side of the dry land over which Israel could walk, so that the Egyptians could not go around Israel, but could only follow after them.

After midnight the Israelites began to cross over where the sea had been. As the night wore on, the Egyptians pursued them. Their chariot wheels stuck in the wet sand, however, making progress slow so that they drove with difficulty. About dawn, at Yahweh's command, Moses again stretched out his staff over the sea, and the waters returned to their former flow. The Egyptians were caught in midcourse and were drowned in the waters. When the sun broke over the land, Israel looked back and saw the dead bodies of the Egyptian soldiers floating on the waters. Once more Yahweh had made fools of the oppressors of His people, glorifying His name on the world stage.

Israel was finally free. Moses and the people sang a song of praise to Yahweh by the shores of the Red Sea. Yahweh was their strength and their song, their power in battle, and the joy they had after victory; He had become their salvation and rescue! (Exod. 15:2). Miriam, Aaron's sister,[1] led the women in the praise of God, as they danced and played with timbrels.

Moses, the fugitive who fled arrest and execution in Egypt for killing an Egyptian, the failure of a man who brought only misery to his people after returning to Egypt, was now completely vindicated. "When Israel saw the great power which Yahweh had used against the Egyptians, the people feared Yahweh and they believed in Yahweh and in His servant Moses" (Exod. 14:31). In the eyes of his countrymen,

---

1   She is called "the prophetess" in Exod. 15:20, possibly because she was the sister to the prophets Aaron and Moses, sharing some of their prestige. In the same way the wife of Isaiah the prophet was called "the prophetess" in Isa. 8:3, though there is no record of her every prophesying.

Moses grew to heroic proportions, as their leader and savior. Note the pairing: Israel believed in Yahweh and in His servant Moses." Moses was no longer a man whose authority could be doubted. Behind his word and leadership stood the authority of God Himself. Moses was a true prophet, a man of God.[1]

Moses had successfully brought Israel out of Egypt, and now began to journey to Horeb, to Mount Sinai. As God said (Exod. 3:12), Israel must come to worship Him at that mountain.

Lessons from the Lawgiver's Life

From Israel's passage through the Red Sea, we learn that our deliverance, salvation, and new life come to us as we pass through the water—specifically, the water of baptism. The typological connection of Israel's experience of passing through the cloud and the sea with that of baptism is as old as St. Paul, who referred to this experience as their Mosaic baptism in 1 Corinthians 10:1–4. This connection of Israel's Mosaic baptism with our Christian baptism is strengthened as we read the Old Testament in the original Hebrew, for then we can make other connections as well.

Life always comes through water—water upon which the *ruach* of God has come. The Hebrew word *ruach* can mean "wind," "breath," or "spirit," and usually a combination of all three. Thus, in Ezekiel 37, we read of God's ruach (rendered in the ESV as "breath") coming into the flesh-covered bones, and then of Ezekiel asking *ruach* to come from the four *ruachoth* (rendered in the ESV as "the four winds") into those bodies, and then of God's promise that this vision meant that He would place His *ruach* (rendered in the ESV as "Spirit")

---

1   The term "man of God" means "prophet" (see 1 Sam. 9:6; 1 Kings 12:22, 17:24; 2 Kings 4:7). Moses is referred to as "the man of God" in the heading of Ps. 90.

within them. The word *ruach* contains all meanings.

In Genesis 1:2 we read of God's *ruach* over the primordial waters, so that God first created life out of the waters over which His *ruach* had brooded. In Genesis 8:1 we read that when God began to re-create a new world after the Flood had destroyed all life in the old one, He sent His *ruach* upon the waters. And now here in the Exodus account of Israel's salvation and their creation as a redeemed nation, we also read of God sending His *ruach* upon the waters of the sea (Exod. 14:21). In all three accounts we see God's ruach coming upon the waters to bring new life.

A Christian, especially one baptized in the Orthodox Church, can hardly miss the connection of this passage with his or her baptism. In baptism, Christians pass through the water which God uses as an instrument of His *ruach* or Spirit. (Indeed, in the Orthodox baptismal rite, the priest not only prays for the Spirit to come upon the water, but he actually breathes three times upon the water himself.) Passing through the water means that we leave the old world of sin, slavery, and death behind us, and emerge into a new life in the Promised Land—just as Israel did at the Red Sea.

Satan can chase us right up to the moment when we enter the waters, just as Pharaoh's army did to Israel, but he cannot touch us when we rise from the baptismal font to our new life. Emerging from that font we enter the land of the living, leaving behind our guilty life of sin and our slavery to death once and for all. There will still be foes and giants to encounter and overcome after our baptism, just as Israel had to encounter and overcome gigantic foes once they entered the Promised Land. But, like Israel, we have been promised the victory by our God who saved us when we passed through the Spirit-touched waters.

Part Two

THE TEN WORDS

Day Eleven
The Journey of Grace: Part I

At Marah: Bitter Water Turned Sweet

AFTER CROSSING THROUGH the Red Sea, Moses led Israel through the wilderness of Shur,[1] in the north western Sinai Peninsula[2] heading toward Mount Sinai and their rendezvous with God. After three days of journeying where no water could be found, their water supply was getting low, and it became imperative to find more water. They then came to a place that had water, and thought that here they could slake their thirst, and restore their water supply. But when they tasted the water, it was bitter, and too salty to drink. They feared it would make them sick if they drank it, and they refused to touch it. They even named the place, Marah, meaning bitterness.

In the desert, one's very existence depended upon a water supply, and the people turned on Moses once again. More specifically, they "grumbled at Moses" (Exod. 15:24), which

---

1   The word "Shur" means "wall," referring to the mountainous ridge which runs east–west, marking the beginning of the Tih Plateau in the peninsula.

2   Gen. 25:18 and 1 Sam. 15:7 place it "opposite Egypt," ruling out a location further east in Edom or Midian.

was not simply a muttering under their breath, but a loud and violent threatening. The same word is used in Exod. 17:3–4, at which Moses cried to the Lord in fear, "What shall I do to this people? A little more and they will stone me!" For the Israelites, the crisis at this deceiving oasis was a matter of life and death, and they blamed Moses for their impending doom.

As Moses cried to Yahweh for help, Yahweh "showed him a tree, and he threw it into the waters, and the waters became sweet"—i.e., safe and drinkable. The word here rendered "showed" is connected with the root for the word "instruction," in Hebrew, "torah," making a clear connection of Yahweh's instruction for Moses regarding the tree and the Torah (or Law) He would later reveal.

This is made clearer still in Yahweh's promise which follows: "If you will give heed to the voice of Yahweh your God and give ear to His commandments and keep all His statutes, I will put none of the diseases on you which I have put on the Egyptians, for I am Yahweh your healer." When Moses obeyed Yahweh's instruction, potentially disease-laden water was healed and made safe for drinking. This illustrates what God would do for Israel in the Promised Land: if the nation would obey His instruction and Law, it would be spared the diseases and plagues which befell Egypt. Yahweh came to save, heal, and bless His people. Their nation could avoid plagues, droughts, and famines—but only if they obeyed His Law. At the waters of Marah,[1] God taught Israel by example and action, as He would later teach them by law and precept.

At the Wilderness of Sin: Bread from Heaven

After more journeying, Israel left the wilderness of Shur and entered the wilderness of Sin, in the southwest of the Sinai

---

[1]   The name "*Marah*" was the name later given by Israel to this oasis, since in Hebrew "*marah*" means "bitter."

Peninsula. Once again, they grumbled against Moses and Aaron, and contemplated rejecting their leadership and their destination. They had begun to run out of food and imagined that Moses and Aaron would let them die of hunger in the wilderness. "Would that we had died by Yahweh's hand in the land of Egypt, when we sat by pots of meat, when we ate bread to the full, for you have brought us out into this wilderness to kill this whole assembly with hunger!" By the phrase "dying by Yahweh's hand in the land of Egypt" they meant dying along with the Egyptians on the night of the Passover. The complaint showed a tremendous ingratitude for all that Yahweh had done for them—including an insensitivity to the plight of the Egyptian firstborn who had died as a price of their current freedom.

Yahweh bore patiently with such stunning ingratitude, and simply said, "Behold, I will rain bread from heaven for you." But the provision would contain a test of their obedience, to see whether or not they would walk in His instruction (in Hebrew, in His "Torah," or Law): beginning the next morning, God would bring bread from heaven for them every day for six days in a row, including a double amount on the sixth day, but nothing on the seventh day. They were to gather the bread in the morning, about half a gallon[1] apiece for everyone in each of their families. The provision would not last into the evening but would melt when the sun grew hot. On the sixth day they were to gather the double amount that God had provided, and they would find that on the seventh day what had been kept aside for use on that day would still be edible—but not what had been kept aside on any other day. On the other days, the food would become foul and bred worms if kept until the next morning. In this way their obedience to God's Sabbath commandment would be tested. Once again God was teaching His people by His miraculous actions among them, as well as by verbal precept.

---

1   In Hebrew measures, a homer.

When the people went out the next morning, they found it even as Yahweh had said—a fine white flake-like substance covered the ground. It tasted like honey. When they first saw it, they were puzzled, and said, "What's this?" (In Hebrew *man hu?*), for which reason it was later called "manna." Moses kept some in a jar as a permanent testimony to God's care for Israel in the wilderness.

What was this manna? A number of commentators have called attention to a desert phenomenon whereby certain kinds of aphids which lived on the tamarisk trees of the region absorbed the sugar from the trees and exuded from their bodies sugar in the form of dry whitish globules, which were available in the early morning. It is possible that God used this phenomenon as the basis for His supernatural feeding of the people. The phenomenon itself was not sufficient to account for the miraculous feeding, since the food from the aphids was not available in double amounts every six days, and did not retain its edibility on the seventh day in a way that was any different from the other six days of the week. It would seem that God used the phenomena of the desert as the material for His miraculous and supernatural provision.

At Meribah: Water from the Rock

At length the Israelites camped at Rephidim and found no water there. It is possible that Rephidim was an oasis, so that they expected to find water and were thus the more distressed at finding the oasis dry.[1] The people "grumbled against Moses," contended with him and demanding that he give them water. As in Exod. 15:24, this "grumbling" was no mere muttering, but an open challenge to Moses' authority to lead—now so severe, after their difficulties over finding water at Marah and bread in the wilderness, that Moses

---

[1]   Perhaps the stream had gone dry, since the dry summer months had come.

feared that they would stone him, and Moses cried out to Yahweh in fear of his life.

In response Yahweh commanded Moses to take the staff of his authority and stand at a prominent crag "on the rock of Horeb"[1] and strike the crag with his staff to make water come from the craggy rock. Though it is possible that water-saturated rocks might produce a stream of water,[2] this does not negate God's providence toward Moses in showing exactly where to strike. What is clear is that Yahweh's word to Moses showed that Yahweh was able to provide miraculous care for His people and provide water even in the desert.

After this, Moses named the place in which this test of their faith and their challenge to his authority occurred "Massah and Meribah," because there they tested Yahweh and argued with Moses—the words "Massah" and "Meribah" meaning "testing" and "argument."[3]

— *Lessons from the Lawgiver's Life*

From these occasions of Israel's testing as they journeyed to Sinai we learn several things.

First of all, we learn from Israel's experience at Marah how God saves us through a tree. When Moses threw the wood of the tree into the water which Israel feared would bring disease and death, that water was changed so that it could give life.

---

1   The reference to Horeb indicates that Israel was already in the wilderness of Horeb in which Mount Sinai could be found.

2   For a possible explanation, see "Science and the Miracles of Exodus," Colin Humphreys, Department of Materials Science & Metallurgy, Cambridge, UK in *Europhysics News,* May/June, 2005.

3   A double place name was unusual. It is possible that the text means that Moses simply named the place "Meribah" (i.e., "Argument") since it was a place of testing (Hebrew "massah"). In Ps. 95:8 we read that the place was called "Meribah," for in this place occurred a "day of testing [Hebrew *massah*] in the wilderness."

In its original Old Testament context, the tree at Marah would be identified with "the tree of life"—i.e., the divine wisdom contained in God's Law (Prov. 3:18). This identification is consistent with the play on words in Exod. 15:25, where the stem of the verb used for producing water (*yarah*) connects with the noun *torah* (meaning "law, instruction"). Israel always thought of the Law as the epitome of divine wisdom. Thus, in Baruch 3:35–4:1, we read of God's wisdom "appearing on earth, and living among men"—i.e., as "the Book of the commandments of God, the Law that endures forever." The Law was the eternal wisdom of God, living with Him in the heavens, and revealed to Israel on earth—a true tree of life for all who embraced it.

In the New Testament we find that the divine Wisdom, eternal with the Father (Prov. 8:22ff.) really did appear on earth and live among men—Jesus of Nazareth, the eternal Word and Wisdom of God. Christ's cross truly became the tree of life for us, for the wood of that cross changes death into life for those who accept Him as the wisdom of God (1 Cor. 1:24). We who drink iniquity like water (Job 15:16) need such a tree of life, so that we can find life in the midst of this sinful and death-dealing world.

Secondly, we learn from Israel's experiences with the heavenly manna to live in daily trust and obedience to God. God provided Israel's daily bread, but the provision was not given all at once, but every day, so that Israel could learn to look every day to God to provide what they needed. The manna could not be stored up overnight or hoarded for future consumption (except on the sixth night, in anticipation of their obedience on the seventh day). Each day offered a new opportunity to trust God to provide for them. It is the same with us in the desert of the world—each new day we must look to God to provide what is truly needed. The stresses and strains of living in the secular desert tempt us to doubt that God will provide, and to worry about tomorrow. The daily provision of our manna from God bids us to resist this temptation. If God feeds the birds of the air, will He not also feed us His children? We need not worry about tomorrow (Matt. 6:26, 34), for God's mercies are new every morning (Lam. 3:22–23).

Finally, we learn from Israel's experience at Meribah of the danger of hardening our hearts. By David's time, the day of testing at Meribah had become an image of Israel's hard-hearted rebellion against God—a rebellion which resulted in their failure to enter into God's rest (Ps. 95:11). As the writer of the Book of Hebrews later observed, this "rest" to which David referred could not simply mean rest in the Promised Land. It is true that the generation of Meribah did not enter Canaan but died in the wilderness. Yet, Israel had long since entered Canaan by the time David wrote Psalm 95, and yet David still warned of the danger of hardening one's heart. By this it was clear that the "rest" meant not just entry into Canaan, but entry into the heavenly rest of God, when at life's end we finally rest from our works in our heavenly home (Heb. 4:1–10). Since the promise of entering into God's rest remains for us, we must beware lest our hearts grow hard, causing us to drift from our faith, and to fall away from the living God (Heb. 3:12).

Day Twelve
The Journey of Grace: Part II

War with Amalek: Help in Battle

WHILE ISRAEL WAS ENCAMPING at Rephidim, the Amalekites attacked them. The Amalekites were a Bedouin people who lived in the south of Canaan or near Kadesh in the Sinai Peninsula. Their attack on Israel was not a defensive move against the Israelite invaders (as Exod. 17:8 states that they "came and fought against Israel"—i.e., came from elsewhere). Rather, as with Bedouin tribes generally, such raiding was part of their way of life, a violent series of aggressive forays for the purpose of plunder. Although the Israelites had little experience of warfare, Moses said to Joshua that he should choose whatever men he could find at such short notice to defend Israel and fight against Amalek. He would station himself atop a local hill to pray for victory, taking the staff of God with him.

Joshua went forth to find the best men he could from the untrained former slaves of Egypt. Moses went forth to the hill with Aaron and Hur[1] to pray for victory. Moses lifted up

---

1   Hur, like Joshua, had not been mentioned in the narrative thus far. Later interpretation would identify Hur as the husband of Moses' sister Miriam—a mere speculation, but as reasonable a guess as any other.

his hands in prayer (the normal posture for prayer), holding his staff in his hand, and as long as he maintained his posture of intercession, Israel prevailed over Amalek. When Moses' hands sunk down due to fatigue, Amalek prevailed over Israel. Given this, Aaron and Hur positioned themselves at either side of Moses who seated himself upon a rock, while Aaron and Hur stood on either side and held his prayerful hands aloft until the final victory over Amalek was won.

After the victory, Yahweh commanded Moses to make a permanent memorial [Hebrew *zikkaron*] of this victory as a reminder that Israel must maintain unrelenting hostility to Amalek in the succeeding generations until they were destroyed. The words often rendered "Write this in a book or scroll" (Hebrew "in a *sepher*"; Exod. 17:14) could equally well be rendered, "Write this as an inscription." If this was the case, Yahweh's commandment was fulfilled when "Moses built an altar and named it, 'Yahweh our banner'" (v. 15).[1] That is, on this altar Moses inscribed the words, "*Yahweh nisi*"—"Yahweh our banner"—i.e., Yahweh is the One around whom we gather in battle.

The Hebrew word *nisi*—often translated "banner"—means "pole," such as the poles or standards around which tribes gathered for battle (e.g., Isa. 5:26). In this interpretation, the altar which Moses erected served as a permanent reminder[2] of Israel's victory over Amalek, and of their commitment to perpetual war against them until they were blotted out from under heaven. The altar (not a scroll) served as the *zikkaron* that Israel must regard Amalek as their eternal

---

[1] If one interprets the commandment as telling Moses to later write a volume to commemorate the victory, one wonders why the text says that Moses fulfilled the commandment not by writing a book, but by building an altar.

[2] The word in Hebrew is *zikkaron*, "memorial," found also in Josh. 4:7 where it described the permanent reminder of Israel's crossing over the Jordan and of their mandate to conquer the Canaanites they found there.

foe, and Moses must let Joshua, as his successor, know of the significance of this altar. Israel's battles were just beginning, but they could expect divine aid from Yahweh to give them victory.

Meeting with Jethro: Help in Judging

After this victory in battle, Moses visited his father-in-law Jethro. Jethro of course had heard the news of the Hebrews' liberation from Egypt and their journey southward toward Horeb, and he went to meet Moses along with his daughter Zipporah and their two children. It would seem that Moses sent Zipporah and their children[1] away from Egypt when things began to become dangerous. The fact that this was not narrated is hardly surprising in a narrative which neglected to give either the names of Moses' sister Miriam or (his possible brother-in-law) Hur. The main protagonist remained Yahweh, and Moses and his family were secondary.

When Jethro met Moses, Moses paid him the respect that their culture expected of a son-in-law to his father-in-law and prostrated himself before him, and then told him all the wonderful things which Yahweh their God had done since they had parted in Midian.

Jethro quickly noticed how Moses' time was consumed by the tasks of judging between his people in minor civil suits and domestic quarrels, and that he was occupied with this task from morning to evening. As a man of experience, Jethro advised Moses that this practice was not good, because it would eventually wear him out. He advised him to appoint other men to help him with this work, men who were honest (and would therefore refuse bribes), and leave these men to

---

[1]   Moses' second son was called "Eliezer"—"my God is my help"—a very Hebrew name, and perhaps a sign that Moses continued to identify with His Hebrew people prior to his departure from Midian.

judge the lesser cases, leaving only the weightier cases for Moses to judge. Being a man of meekness and humility, "Moses listened to the voice of his father-in-law and did all that he said" (Exod. 18:24). Through this, God not only gave Israel victory over their external foes such as Amalek, but over their internal disunity. Israel remained at peace, both without and within.

— Lessons from the Lawgiver's Life

Moses' posture with his uplifted hands of intercession is an image of victory. The position of his hands was decisive: when his hands sunk down, Israel experienced defeat, and when his hands were lifted up, Israel experienced victory. The text does not connect Moses' posture with his people's determination to fight, but with the victory given (or withheld) by God: hands upheld in prayer meant that God would give victory, and when he dropped his prayerful hands, victory was forfeited. The immediate lesson for Israel was plain: future victory over their foes was assured if only they would trust God and look to Him in prayer.

For Christians, this narrative contains a further lesson, since the image of victory was that of Moses on a hill at sunset with his arms outstretched. Christians could hardly forget their own Savior upon the hill as the day declined, with His own hands outstretched on the cross, giving victory over Satan and death. For Christians this posture of Moses, sustained throughout the day as the sign and giver of victory, could hardly fail to remind them of the posture of Christ upon His cross throughout that saving day. Israel's perpetual battle against Amalek, preserved for all generations by the erection of the inscribed altar, imaged the Christian's perpetual battle against Satan. As with Moses, victory for the Christians was assured by the outstretched arms of their leader upon the hill.

As well as the help God gave Israel over their external foes from without, we see a lesson in the help God gave Israel over the internal forces of disunity from within. God appointed leaders within Israel to share Moses' authority and to share his work of judging the people. In the same way, God appointed leaders within His Church to share Christ's authority. As the Lord said to His apostles, "He who receives you receives Me" (Matt. 10:40), so that the leaders and clergy of the Church share in the authority of Christ Himself. It is true that there is a radical egalitarianism in the Church, so that no one functions as a guru or an authority in himself, but that all are the disciples of Christ (Matt. 23:8–10). It is also true that Christ shares His authority with men, so that some of His disciples function as leaders with authority over others (Heb. 13:17). The Church is an ordered community, containing leaders with authority, and rejecting this authority involves rejecting the authority of Christ who gave this authority to others for the common good.

Day Thirteen
Meeting God

Preparation

THREE MONTHS AFTER ISRAEL had left Egypt, they departed from the wilderness of Sin[1] and entered the wilderness of Sinai, to the place which God had commanded Moses to bring His people after He had set them free. He had brought them to Sinai before bringing them into the Promised Land because they could only conquer that land after they had become God's covenant people through whom He could manifest His power. And that covenant was established on Mount Sinai.

God began by calling Moses to ascend Mount Sinai so that He could speak with him and send him down to Israel as His ambassador. The covenant He proposed was simple in its essence: He had already demonstrated His power and His care for them in bringing them out of Egypt and keeping them safe in the wilderness. If they would listen to God and keep His covenant, they would become His special possession, a kingdom of priests with unique access to His presence among all the peoples of the earth, a nation set apart from

---

[1] "Sin" is not etymologically related to the Old English word, sin, but rather bears reference to the moon, likely a semitic moon goddess.

all others (Exod. 19:4–6). Moses descended the mountain to bring this proposal to the elders of the people, and they formally assented to enter into this covenant: "All that Yahweh has spoken we will do!" Moses then re-ascended the mountain to bring Yahweh word of their acceptance of the covenant and its terms.

God then said that He Himself would personally descend upon Mount Sinai, granting them a theophany that He might speak with them face to face. When they heard God's voice, this would seal forever Moses' authority as His representative in the eyes of his people. Preparation was needed to meet God. They must spend that day and the next consecrating themselves by entering a state of ritual purity through washing their clothes[1] and abstain from sexual intercourse.[2] The mountain onto which God was to descend became holy and therefore off limits, like the (later) Holy of Holies in the Tabernacle. The mountain was to be set off with markers of some kind, and animals restrained from entering there to graze. If an animal did trespass onto holy ground, it was to be shot with arrows, not retrieved, nor killed by someone also trespassing upon the mountain. The mountain was thus to be sacrosanct while Yahweh rested upon it. Israel would be summoned to the foot of the mountain to meet their God when they heard the supernatural blast of a ram's horn. Even as such horns were used to summon and direct armies, so Yahweh's hosts would be summoned to meet Him with the horn's blast when they were ready.

---

1   A difficult process in the desert with limited water, thus requiring two days.
2   By "ritual purity" is meant the avoidance anything which would render one ritually unclean, such as touching dead bodies. Sexual intercourse also rendered one ritually impure (compare 1 Sam. 21:4). There was no ethical element whatsoever involved; neither contact with the dead nor sexual intercourse were morally wrong.

Theophany at Sinai

When God first appeared to Moses in the Sinai wilderness, a small bush had burned with the fire of God's presence. Now the entire mountain was the fiery conflagration that signaled the presence of the living God. On the morning of the third day, a thick cloud of darkness enveloped the mountain, which began to shake violently in the presence of Yahweh. There was continuous thunder and lightning atop the mountain, and thick smoke enveloped it, like the thick smoke escaping from a furnace. A trumpet sounded, announcing the arrival of Yahweh, its sound growing louder and louder. Moses spoke to God, and God answered him with a voice which thundered loud enough to be heard over the terrifying din.

Thus did Yahweh, the God of Abraham, Isaac, and Jacob, descend in fire upon the top of Mount Sinai, and summoned Moses to meet with him at its summit for a private audience. Israel remained below, trembling in fear. (The theophany was so terrifying that afterward Israel begged that He speak to them directly no more—after this, let God speak to Moses privately, and let him convey to them the words of God.) The principle of mediating prophets in Israel dates from this time. Hearing directly from God proved too much for them.

In Moses' audience with Yahweh at the summit of Sinai, Yahweh told Moses once again of the importance of Israel remaining at a safe distance, lest they be consumed if they broke through the barrier and insisted on approaching God unsummoned and uninvited. God's holiness did not allow for such presumption. At a later time, He would allow the priests[1] to come for an audience, but even they had to consecrate themselves to make themselves ready, and Aaron also at length would be summoned. Before God would address His people at large, He took care to keep them safe and separate.

---

[1] Since the priesthood had not yet been set apart for the tribe of Levi, it appears that the elders of the people are here intended (see Exod. 18:12; 24:1, 5, 9).

After this, Moses descended the mountain again and stood with his people to hear the words of God from His own mouth. Those words spoken into the ears of His trembling people consisted of ten words,[1] i.e. ten messages. He had set them free from the slavery of Egypt so that they could become a kingdom of priests; here were ten ways to preserve that freedom and live as priests should live.

Lessons from the Lawgiver's Life

From the elaborate precautions surrounding Yahweh's arrival on Mount Sinai we may gain insight into how fearful a thing it is to enter the presence of the living God. Our apostate and secularized Western culture has lost all notion of the fear of God. We imagine that God, if He exists, may be approached as easily and casually as any one of our neighbors might be approached, or as a stranger in the street. More awe attends entering the presence of an earthly monarch (such as the Queen of England), or a Hollywood celebrity, or even the office of our own boss than we often think should attend entry into the presence of Almighty God. Even Moses, though summoned to His presence by the spectacle of the burning bush, was warned to come only so far and no further, and then to remove the sandals from his feet.

The awe and difficulty which truly attends entering the presence of God is well expressed by part of a prayer which the priest quietly offers for himself in the Orthodox Divine Liturgy: "No one who is bound with the desires and pleasures of the flesh is worthy to approach or draw near or to serve You, O King of glory, for to minister to You is great and awesome even to the heavenly powers." Anyone can offer

---

1   The Hebrew does not speak of "ten commandments," but "ten words" (Hebrew *dabarim*) (Exod. 34:28; Deut. 10:4). The Greek Septuagint translates it accurately as the ten "*remata* or *logous*" (both being the Greek terms for "words".)

prayer, of course, but drawing near to God's presence to commune with Him (the essence of worship, such as the worship at the Mosaic Tabernacle, of Solomon's Temple, or at the Christian Divine Liturgy) is something different than merely uttering a prayer which God hears from heaven. Drawing near to God requires daring from sinful man.

How then do we Christians dare to draw near to God in worship? Only through the blood of Christ. Christ offered Himself on the cross, and His blood cleanses the cosmos— both things on earth and things in heaven (Col. 1:20; Heb. 9:23). After His death and resurrection, Christ ascended into heaven itself (of which the Mosaic shrine was a mere copy and type), preparing the way for us. We now have confidence to draw near to God's throne and find grace by the blood of Jesus (Heb. 4:16; 10:19). Of course, we draw near in repentance and humility, having been baptized and washed with pure water, and having our hearts sprinkled clean from an evil conscience (Heb. 10:22). Something is required from us as well, so that we come to God having repented of our sins and having forgiven our debtors. But ultimately our access into the presence of God now depends not upon our own personal merits, but on the mercy of God and the blood of His Christ. Our growth and spiritual health depend upon our never losing sight of this, and of the immensity of the privilege of drawing near to the living God, the consuming fire, the terror of Sinai.

Day Fourteen
The Ten Words

The First Word (Exod. 20:2–3)

The first word God spoke to Israel on Sinai was:

> "I am Yahweh your God, who brought you out of the
> land of Egypt, out of the house of slavery. You shall
> have no other gods before Me."

WE SEE IN THIS FIRST WORD how the "Ten Words" differ from "Ten Commandments." A commandment can be construed as a demand, a condition set by God which must be fulfilled before He will offer acceptance and love. This is too often how our secular generation regards these ten words, or any of God's words to us—as the more or less arbitrary requirements of a severe and unforgiving deity, and as the basis upon which God will show Himself as a God of love. When we hear, "You shall be holy, for I am holy" (Lev. 11:45; 1 Pet. 1:15–16), we hear it as a demand which must be first obeyed before God will deign to touch us.

But that is not true. God had already showed His love and care for Israel before they had ever reached Sinai. He had brought them out of the land of Egypt, out of the house of slavery; He had saved them at the Red Sea; He had turned bitter water into sweet water; He had given them quails to eat one evening and manna from heaven to eat every morning. He had brought water from the flinty rock—and all this despite their ceaseless grumbling and rebellion, their ingratitude, their repeated faithlessness. The journey from the sea to the Sinai was thus a journey of grace. His entire relationship with Israel was one of undeserved grace, compassion, care, and kindness. He had proven abundantly over and over again that He loved them and was a God of love. Fulfilling the ten words were not Israel's way of earning His love, as it is clear that He already loved them, and that such striving was not necessary. Fulfilling the ten words were to be Israel's way of loving Him back.[1]

The call to "have no other gods before Me" (literally, "before My face"—as if the sight of such rivals was a provocation) reveals that what God wants from us is not simply ethical behavior, but our hearts. When God gave to Israel the ten words, polytheism was the accepted norm. A person or group might have their favorite deity, but it was understood that all deities were entitled to some worship, and that no deity could claim the exclusive worship of his or her devotee.

Indeed, some people defined piety as giving to all the deities their devotional due and leaving none of them without some form of worship (thus the Athenians later erected an altar to an "To the Unknown God" just in case a deity was inadvertently ignored and sent a plague upon the city as a result; see Acts 17:23). The temptation was to decide that "when in Rome (or Canaan) do as the Romans (or Canaanites) do," and worship their gods as well. In this thinking, the worship of Yahweh would then not be replaced by the

---

1 Later developments in Judaism, such as the views of some of the Pharisees, would distort this understanding, and transform the Law into a heavy yoke. It was this distortion that St. Paul was addressing in his epistles (which should not be read as his commentary on the original intent and purpose of the Law).

worship of such Canaanite gods as Baal, but only augmented. Such an expansion of the Hebrew pantheon to include gods other than Yahweh was not regarded as sinful idolatry, but as broadminded and generous ecumenism.

Yahweh did not regard it thus. The other gods were not gods like Him, or even gods somewhat inferior to Him. They were not gods at all, but demons (Deut. 32:17; 1 Cor. 10:20), and the rites by which they were worshiped—which included "sacred" prostitution, both male and female, and child sacrifice—were often abominable. Israel must therefore refuse to worship them at all, and when their altars and sacred sites were discovered after Israel entered Canaan, they were to be smashed and demolished so that the sacrifices to those gods could not continue (Exod. 34:13).

This freedom from spiritual contamination by these demonic "gods" was the reason why Israel was to refuse intermarriage with the Canaanites—an intermarriage made more difficult by different food laws from them.[1]

This demonic element in the worship of the Canaanite gods therefore necessitated Israel's separation from them, both culturally and religiously. This latter went against everything they had been taught in polytheistic Egypt and in the world at large. No other god objected if his or her devotee worshiped other gods as well. As long as the devotee fed that god by offering sacrifice, the god had no objection to their devotee feeding and worshiping other gods as well. Because this instinct was so ingrained in the cultures of that day, overruling it and insisting upon a devotional exclusivity became the very first word that Yahweh spoke to His people. If they became demoniacally infected, there was little remedy for it. After the coming of Jesus Christ, the people of

---

1   The reason for banning of certain foods was not hygienic or moral (or allegorical), but social: if an Israelite could not eat pork, for example, their family could not socialize with the Canaanites who did. The food laws served to keep Israel culturally separate—and therefore spiritually safe.

God possessed the authority to cast out the demons with a word and liberate and heal the infected person (Luke 10:17), but no such authority or remedy existed then. Healing the demon-infected person was difficult or impossible; the only alternative therefore was prevention in the first place. Thus the Law is replete with counsels that insist upon Israel's separation from the demon-infested world.

This word has lost none of its relevance today, even in places where polytheism or the demonic is not acknowledged as real. Mankind is a race addicted to idolatry, and determined to find alternatives to the living God. We may no longer choose Baal as an alternative to God, or any of the multitude of deities which filled the ancient world. We may no longer acknowledge the reality of the existence of demons, but we still insist upon choosing something other than God as the effective and unifying center of our lives. And whatever we choose as this center is, by definition, our god, our idol.

St. Paul is clear about this. When he was warning his readers to flee sins, he mentioned the sin of covetousness. To covet something is not simply to desire it; it is to insist on having what someone else has. If I covet your car (say for example your Porsche), I do not want a Porsche like yours or identical to yours: I want your Porsche. If I covet your wife, I do not want a wife like her, but her. To covet something therefore is to make what is coveted into an idol—for which reason St. Paul writes that covetousness is idolatry (Eph. 5:5; Col. 3:5).

There are thus many ways of embracing idolatry. Our Lord Jesus speaks of the pursuit of wealth as an idol, giving this the name "Mammon," which He says sets itself up as a rival with God for our affection. Like God, Mammon demands all our heart and all our devotion. We therefore cannot serve both God and Mammon, for the same reason that a person cannot be the slave of two masters: each master claim total ownership over the slave, so that the slave has to choose which master he will be owned by and will serve (Matt. 6:24; Luke 16:13). If the Father is our true God, we will serve Him with all our heart, the way that a slave serves his master. If Mammon is our true God, we will serve Mammon with all our heart, with true devotion.

The point is this: in this world, Mammon is a god, though he is not the only deity claiming devotion from his worshipers. Fame, sexual gratification, and other sensual pleasures also present themselves as ultimately desirable, and as paths to true fulfillment—in other words, as gods. Even after western secularization, the world is still stuffed full of gods. God's first word to His people has lost none of its relevance: "I am Yahweh your God. You shall have no other gods before Me."

Day Fifteen
The Second Word (Exod. 20:4–6)

The second word God spoke to Israel on Sinai was:

> "You shall not make for yourself a carved image or any likeness of what is in heaven above, or in the earth beneath, or in the water under the earth. You shall not prostrate to them nor serve them. For I, Yahweh your God, am a jealous God, visiting the iniquity of the fathers upon the sons to the third and fourth generations of those who hate Me, but showing covenant-loyalty to thousands, to those who love Me and keep My commandments."

THIS SECOND WORD also presupposes the religious culture of the day, in which a deity was not real unless one could see its physical image in its temple. The word here rendered "carved image" is the Hebrew word *pesel*, cognate with the Hebrew word for "carving," whether the carving be of wood or stone. The idea was that the deity had reality and was present in this world through its visible image. A god which had no visible carved image had no real existence in this world. That image must be commensurate with the deity itself. Thus, a deity of power and fertility might be fitly imaged by a carving of a bull-calf, since bulls were animals of strength and fertility. The gods might be considered

as projections and personifications of the forces of nature—
thus the multiplicity of gods in the ancient world.

Yahweh was entirely different from these deities. He could
not be considered the personification of one of the forces of
nature since He was the creator of nature, entirely transcen-
dent and removed far above this physical world. No physical creature could function to serve as His image. The birds
flying in heaven above (like the falcon, whose head served
to image the Egyptian god Horus), or animals in the earth
beneath (like Bastet, who was imaged by a cat), could never
serve to adequately represent Him. No creature could fitly
image Yahweh. Any image could only diminish His glory
and reduce Him to the stature of the creatures He had made,
on par with the gods of the nations—and ultimately to be
worshiped along with them.

Yahweh was "a jealous God." Note: "jealous," not "envi-
ous"—He was jealous in the godly way that a husband is jealous of the love of his wife. Like the jealous husband, Yahweh
will not allow His people to reduce Him to the status of one
of the forces of nature, as were the other pagan gods. His jealousy was rooted in His care for His people, not in ego. Making Yahweh like just another pagan god was iniquitous, and
such iniquity in a family would be visited with punishment
by all who indulged in it—not just the grandfather of the
family, but the grandfather's son, and his grandson, and his
great-grandson. As many generations in the family as tried to
idolatrously portray Yahweh in the way the pagan gods were
portrayed would suffer for their sins, for such idolatry meant
that they "hated" or rejected Yahweh. But to those who remained faithful and who acknowledged that He was different than the gods of the nations would be blessed by Him
and would experience His covenant-loyalty[1] though there be
thousands of them. He would bless them all.

One might imagine that our own culture which does not

---

1   Hebrew *hesed*, sometimes rendered "loving-kindness" or "mercy."

use carved images in the worship of its idols and deities has little need of this word. But the temptation to reduce God to a convenient size where He is less threatening is perennial. In our popular culture this temptation is present in its portrayal of God as an old man in a white robe with a long beard. Yet, even the sophisticated majority who realize the comic dimensions of such a portrayal of God still try, with remarkable determination, to reduce Him to such a size where He can be imagined and portrayed.

When we imagine that God is one being among many—the first cause and prime mover perhaps, but still nonetheless one who exists in the same way that His creatures exist and who can be conceived of as not existing—we are guilty of reducing God to the status of a god like the gods of paganism. Yahweh—the eternal I Am—therefore becomes a Judeo-Christian version of Zeus. Not surprisingly, such a god does nothing to compel belief among thoughtful people—nor should He. For such a god is not God, and He is not the God of the Christians.

The Christian God is the God who surpasses every category, including the categories of "being" and "not being." He does not exist in the same that His creatures exist but transcends such categories. One can speak of Him and ascribe qualities to Him (so-called "cataphatic theology"), and meaningfully affirm that God is love, that He is just, that He is merciful, but this must be balanced by "apophatic theology," an understanding that God is too great to be bound by such affirmations. Human language and conceptual statements utterly fail to describe Him. The best response to His presence is not description, but silent wonder and awestruck adoration.

Even among Christians there have been many who are slow to realize this. Even when some do not believe that God is an old man in the sky with a white robe and a long beard, they still cannot resist visualizing Him somehow, and forming conceptual constructs that they feel can adequately describe Him. The path of wisdom, marked out for us by this second word, bids us regard whatever conceptual image we may have of God as inevitable, but inevitably inadequate. As C. S. Lewis once intuited, we must "consciously direct our prayers 'Not to what I think thou art but to what thou knowest thyself to be.'" We must fling aside our thoughts and images of God, or, if we retain them, must do so "with a full recognition of their merely subjective nature," trusting ourselves "to the completely real, external, invisible Presence,"[1] He that is never knowable by us as we are known by Him.

If we mistake our human conceptions of God for God as He truly is, we embrace folly, burden our apologetic proclamation of the Gospel with unnecessary baggage, and transgress against the second word that God spoke to Israel. Sometimes the first step of an unbeliever toward knowing the true and living God is decisively rejecting the reduced and false images of God which he has, which he may mistake for true Christianity.

If such a person imagines that the God of Christianity is a God who lives in the sky, who has an existence like everyone else has (what theologians have called "contingent existence"—a being who conceivably might not have existed), and is a God who damns everyone who has not been baptized, or who has not "been born again" as defined by television evangelists, or who does not read the Bible in the King James Version with the words of Christ in printed in red ink—if such a person rejects that God, he is not necessarily thereby rejecting the true God. The god whom he imagines and rejects is not the true God who actually exists. Rejecting this false God may possibly be the first step toward finding the true God.

The true God of the Bible who has revealed Himself in the Scriptures is a larger deity than that. He cannot be jammed

1   C. S. Lewis, *The Screwtape Letters* (Glasgow: Collins Fount Paperbacks, 1982), pp. 27–28.

into such a small conceptual box. To imagine that He can is to create an idol, an image which cannot adequately represent Him. This second word bids us to enlarge our hearts and our minds, and to recognize our limitations. We come to God not as we imagine Him to be, but to Him as He knows Himself to be. We must resist the temptation to erect mental and conceptual images of God which limit Him and remake Him in our own image.

Day Sixteen
The Third Word (Exod. 20:7)

The third word God spoke to Israel on Sinai was:

> "You shall not take the name of Yahweh your God
> in vain, for Yahweh will not hold him guiltless who
> takes His name in vain."

IN UNDERSTANDING THIS WORD, we must remember
that in the ancient world a name was not simply a verbal
label. Rather it expressed the essential characteristics of
the person and was synonymous with the person himself. To
mention a person's name was to make that person present in
some way—for which reason the Law forbade Israel to have
even the name of the foreign gods upon their lips (Exod.
23:13). To mention a god's name in an oath therefore was
to summon that god as a witness to the oath, with the understanding that the god would take revenge upon the one
taking the oath if the oath was not fulfilled. To "swear falsely"
involved swearing by a god and then not performing what
one had sworn to perform.

This word forbids using the name of Yahweh in this way,
invoking Him in an oath and then not performing the promised action. It was not the only way to take Yahweh's name in
vain—this word also forbids using His name as parts of magical formulas or in magical amulets and talismans, as was the

common practice among the pagans of the time. Common to all these misuses of God's name was the idea of manipulating God, and using His name (that is, using Him) to achieve one's own plans. Reverence for Yahweh involves using His name reverently, and not reducing Him by attempts at verbal manipulation through the use of His name.

The personal name of God, Yahweh, is no longer used in our western culture. Accustomed to monotheism, we no longer regard our God as one deity among many, and for us the name "God" indicates someone unique. For us, if one properly understands the meaning of the word "God," one also understands that it cannot be rendered in the plural. For us the "God" (with the capital letter "G") is by definition different than the plural "gods" (with the uncapitalized letter "g"), so that we feel that someone writing, "I believe in god" has made a spelling error by spelling it without the capital "G." "God" is the unique being who made the world, the one and only true deity; the "gods" are false deities worshiped by the unenlightened ancient pagans. God is unique and *unpluralizable* (to coin a word); He needs no personal name to distinguish Him from the other gods, because there are no other (true) gods from which to distinguish Him.

This being so in the West, in what way is this third word still relevant to us, since we no longer refer to our deity as "Yahweh," but simply as "God?" I suggest that, for Christians, it is still relevant because God does have a personal name, one which distinguishes Him from others. It is not "Yahweh"; it is "Jesus."

In first century Palestine, the name "Jesus" was given to many children, since it was the name of Moses' eminent successor, Yehoshua or Yeshua. (The name of Moses' successor is usually Anglicized as "Joshua" to distinguish it from the "Jesus" of the Gospels.)[1] Because the eternal Logos became

---

1   Except in the King James Version of Heb. 4:8. The name "Yeshua" was rendered in Greek as "Iesous," in Latin as "Iesus," and in English as "Jesus."

incarnate as Yeshua or Jesus, that name contains great power in the mouth of His people. Jesus sent His disciples out to preach and to do miracles as His representatives—that is, in His name. They returned to Him afterward, declaring excitedly, "Lord, even the demons are subject to us in Your name!" (Luke 10:17), and ever afterward the Church has invoked the name of Jesus, in personal prayer, corporate worship, with the affect of even working miracles and exorcisms (Acts 3:6–8; 16:18).

Of course, it was the Christians' faith in Jesus and their authority as His disciples to use that name that counted, as some who were not disciples learned to their cost (Acts 19:13–16). But in the mouth of faithful Christians, pronouncing the name of Jesus in faith was not simply speaking syllables, but invoking the Lord and making Him present. For Christians, the name "Jesus" was not simply another name, but the name which was above every name, the name at which all creation would one day bow (cf. Phil. 2:10–11). The name itself was holy.

This is why the third word spoken by Yahweh on Mount Sinai is still relevant, because in the West the name of Jesus or Jesus Christ is often used as a cuss word, an expletive used along with other expletives when expressing anger or annoyance. Like other expletives, the name has been effectively emptied of meaning and content. When a person is annoyed or angry and he says, "damn!" and the actual meaning of the word does not enter into it. A person saying, "Damn!" does not wish the object of their anger to be endowed with a soul and condemned to perdition. Usually such a person does not even believe in the reality of perdition or damnation.

It is the same with other expletives—the actual meaning of the words carry no meaning in the situation in which they are used. Some expletives are worse than others, in the sense that uttering some words results in greater shock in those that hear them. But all expletives share an identical absence of real meaning. They all mean only one thing—that the person uttering the word is angry or annoyed (or perhaps is simply trying to be emphatic and possesses an impoverished vocabulary).

Here we may see the strategy of the Enemy. The Enemy knows that the name of Jesus, uttered in faith, carries spiritual power, and so by making that name just one more expletive among many, he can effectively empty it of any meaning. A profane person then may utter the sacred and saving name hundreds of times a day and not even know what is coming out of his mouth—the name which alone can save him, the name which is above every name. It is a part of the Enemy's plan to de-sacralize everything in Western culture. The word "Jesus" has been demoted to that of just another meaningless cuss word, just as all Christian words, concepts, and values are being slowly demoted and emptied of relevance. As Christ's disciples, we must resist such a culturally insidious and fatal trend. We must not take the name of Jesus our God in vain.

Day Seventeen
The Fourth Word (Exod. 20:8–11)

The fourth word God spoke to Israel on Sinai was:

> Remember the Sabbath day to keep it holy. Six days
> you shall labor and do all your work, but the sev-
> enth day is the Sabbath[1] to Yahweh your God. In it
> you shall do no work—you, nor your son, nor your
> daughter, nor your male slave, nor your female slave,
> nor your cattle, nor your stranger who is within your
> gates. For in six days Yahweh made the heavens and
> the earth, the sea, and all that is in them, and rested
> the seventh day. Therefore Yahweh blessed the Sab-
> bath day and hallowed it.

THIS WORD ALONE AMONG the ten words has exclu
sively a covenantal, and not moral, significance. That
is, even among the non-Israelite Gentiles, the other
words contain an ethical value. Murder, adultery, and theft
were considered wrong among all the nations of the earth,
even though they were not in covenant with Yahweh. The
other ten words forbade things that were wrong in them-

---

1   The Hebrew word *shabbat* means "cessation," not necessarily rest.
     That is, work must cease after six days regardless of whether or not
     one feels the need for rest.

selves (such as murder), or enjoined things which were right in themselves (such as honoring one's parents). This word alone enjoins something which apart from Yahweh's covenant has no direct moral value.[1]

The Sabbath was a sign of the Mosaic covenant and did not form part of the life of any ancient people before the giving of the Law on Mount Sinai. Abraham and the patriarchs did not keep the Sabbath, nor did Israel when in Egypt.[2] The Sabbath was unique to the Mosaic Law. The closest cultural parallel was the notion of a *shabattu*, a term used by the Babylonians and Assyrians to refer to the day of the full moon, the fifteenth day of the month. Also, the seventh, fourteenth, twenty-first, and twenty-eighth days of the month were significant in the Mesopotamian calendar, being connected with the four phases of the moon. Those days were considered unlucky, so that work done on them might not succeed.

The Mosaic Sabbath, however, was kept regardless of the phases of the moon, and had nothing to do with bad luck. Israel rested on the Sabbath not because work done then might be subject to bad luck, but out of respect for God who had created the world (or, in the later Deuteronomic version of this word, out of respect for God who had brought them out of Egypt; see Deut. 5:15). In this sense, the Mosaic Sabbath was the antithesis of the pagan *shabattu*, for it was not a day of fasting or of misfortune, but a day of rest and of blessing.

---

1   Ceasing from work every seven days has a value to health and life, for working without periodic rest is damaging to one's wellbeing. But the rest enjoined has no moral value: working without rest may be foolish and ill-advised, but it is not sinful in the way that murder, adultery, and theft are sinful.

2   The fourth word connects the Mosaic Sabbath with God's rest after creating the world (Gen. 2:1–3), but the narrative does not imply that God expected neither Adam, nor his descendants to rest on the seventh day. Indeed, there is no Scriptural reference to Sabbath-keeping until the bestowal of the Mosaic Law.

On the seventh day, no unnecessary work was to be done,[1] and one could not cease from work by delegating the work to someone else. Everyone in the family had to cease from work, including children, slaves, and the Gentile sojourner finding shelter with the family. One could not work one's cattle either[2]—all in the family ceased from labor together.

The purpose of the Sabbath was to bind Israel ever closer to God in covenant gratitude. That is why God's creation of the world and His liberation of Israel from Egypt are specified as the rationale for the Sabbath. Every week Israel stopped and remembered that their life on earth and their liberty in the Promised Land came as gifts from Yahweh. The Sabbath functioned as the primary sign and expression of the covenant. What counted in their Sabbath-keeping was not their scrupulosity in avoiding work, but their renewed gratitude and loyalty to God. The Sabbath was to be an affair of the heart, for God wanted relationship above all.

The Sabbath, being a sign of the Mosaic covenant with Israel, had no ethical significance for Gentile Christians. The Church quickly discerned that in Christ they had encountered a reality that transcended religion and the Law, so that "in Christ there is neither circumcision, nor uncircumcision, but a new creation" (Gal. 6:15). In other words, Jewish identity, and with it, the Jewish Law, no longer had covenantal significance. Indeed, after Christ established the new covenant in His blood, the first covenant was made obsolete and ready to disappear (Heb. 8:13). The old Mosaic cove-

---

1   The exaggerated number of restrictions created by the Pharisees and preserved in Rabbinic Judaism are foreign to the spirit of this fourth word. Farm animals must still be fed, lactating animals milked, and the priests still worked in the Mosaic shrine.

2   We note again the strong connection of a man and his beasts in that agrarian culture; compare the death of the firstborn Egyptian cattle related in Exod. 12:29.

nant might retain a merely cultural significance for a Jewish Christian but could have no covenantal significance or binding power for a Gentile Christian. A Jew might still keep the Sabbath, circumcise his male children, and avoid pork, but these things, constitutive as they are for Jewish identity, were now culturally relative and optional.[1]

This being so, of what significance is the Sabbath for members of the Church? The Sabbath was about simple cessation from work, not about prayer or worship. The fourth word contains no command for Israel to pray on the Sabbath, much less offer special worship then, such as they would later in the synagogue. The command was simply to cease from work. But this cessation involved time, and it is this element which retains significance for Christians: as Christians we sanctify time by stopping for prayer—and not just on a particular day.

We stop to pray throughout the day, every day. That of course includes corporate liturgical prayer on Sunday morning, and on the other holy days of the Church's calendar. Christians sanctify time by stopping what they are doing to offer prayer. An early church manual called *The Didache* or *The Teaching of the Twelve Apostles* dating from about 100 A.D. mandated stopping three times a day to say the Lord's Prayer (*The Didache*, chapter 8). The daily hours of 6:00 a.m., 9:00 a.m., noon, and 3:00 p.m. soon became established as

---

1   There is no suggestion in the early Church that Sunday had become the Sabbath, or that the restrictions of the Jewish Sabbath had been transferred to Sunday. The notion of Sunday as the Christian Sabbath is rooted in an attempt to find ethical significance in Sabbath-keeping, since it formed part of the Ten Commandments, which were viewed as possessing eternal moral significance for all time. Sunday is never called "the Sabbath" in the Church. In the Orthodox liturgical calendar, "the Great and Holy Sabbath" is Holy Saturday, not Paschal Sunday.

the normal times for such daily prayers,[1] and after that became standardized in monastic rules as four fixed liturgical
services.[2] Regardless of the system used, we are called upon
to sanctify time by stopping what we are doing to offer prayer
to God and to call Him to be with us in the present moment.
It is true that He will be with us whether or not we invoke
Him, since God is everywhere. What prayer does is bring us
the benefit of communion with Him as we journey through
time. He is always present to us, but we are not always present to Him. Our sanctification depends upon our becoming present to Him, and by offering ourselves to Him in the
midst of our daily life.

---

1   As noted by Tertullian (d. 220 A.D.) in his *On Prayer*, chapter 25.

2   Sometimes these services are grouped together, so that one says the
         Third Hour and the Sixth Hour at about 9:00 a.m. It is rather odd
         and defeats the purpose of interspersing prayer throughout the day.
         One sanctifies the sixth hour (i.e., noon) by praying at the sixth
         hour. Time cannot be sanctified in advance; that is what the very
         idea of "time" means.

Day Eighteen
The Fifth Word (Exod. 20:12)

The fifth word God spoke to Israel on Sinai was:

> "Honor your father and your mother, that your days upon the land which Yahweh your God is giving may be long."

THE MORAL OBLIGATION to honor one's father and mother was taken with great seriousness in the ancient Near East, as it still is taken in such countries of the Middle East today. And it was not just parents who were to be honored, but everyone of the older generation, so that a pious and decent person would "rise up before the hoary head and honor the face of the old man" (Lev. 19:32)—i.e., stand up as a sign of deference when someone with hair white with age entered the room.

This precept in Leviticus 19:32 was followed by the words, "and fear your God: I am Yahweh." In other words, anyone who feared Yahweh would also respect the aged. Respect for parents stood at the center of an entire network of hierarchy and respect. In Israel, for example, a pious son would not offer his own opinion after his father spoke in public, lest he seem to be disagreeing with him. In fact, a pious son would never contradict or criticize his father—especially not in public. Such would have brought shame to the father in that shame-honor culture—to say nothing of the shame brought to the son who publicly dishonored him.

This stands in dramatic contrast to life in the modern West, where old age is largely despised, and where all authority is mocked—especially parental authority. Youth in general feel no obligation whatsoever to honor the aged, and they assume that they have nothing to learn from them. One remembers the words of the grandfather in the movie *Moonstruck*: "I am an old man, and when I speak, my words have no weight." The grandfather in the film speaks for all the aged of the modern West. Our situation is a source of scandal to those raised in the Middle East and in other more traditional cultures—and rightly so.

This fifth word reminds us that everyone finds their place in a hierarchy—in a ladder and on a spiritual map which includes not just human beings, but also plants, animals, and angels. All creatures have their assigned places, and are all entitled to different kinds of respect.[1] Wives are to respect their husbands, husbands are to respect their wives, all are to respect their rulers, the young are to respect the aged, and children are to respect their parents. The command to honor one's parents brings us into the center of a hierarchical world of entitled respect—the direct opposite of our own culture of youthful entitlement and rejection of all hierarchy.

The recognition that everyone finds his place and receives his due honor in a hierarchy brings stability to a society, and becomes the root from which we build on the past. Scientists and learned men know this: each generation of scientists and scholars gratefully receives what the previous generations have accomplished, honors them for those accomplishments, and continues to build on them. Without this honoring of the past, no progress is possible, for then each generation is doomed to start all over again and re-discover (or fail to re-

---

1   Even plants and animals; thus Deut. 20:19, which inculcates respect for trees, and Deut. 22:6–7, which inculcates respect for animals.

discover) what their fathers have discovered. Progress only comes when scholars accept the work that their forefathers in their field have done before them and build upon it—either confirming their conclusions or refuting them and replacing them with others. But either way, the starting point is always where their forefathers have left off.

In other words, science and all scholarship is built upon a foundation of tradition, and tradition finds its root in our willingness to honor what has come before. Honoring our forefathers does not involve blindly accepting their conclusions, but receiving them with gratitude and taking those conclusions as the starting point for further work. We show gratitude to our forefathers for taking us to the place where we are now so that we can take the next steps—and so that those who come after us can receive our work and critically build upon it as we built upon the work of those who came before us.

This word also speaks to us in our life in the Church. Honoring our fathers and mothers involves honoring those through whom God has spoken and given us life in the Church. We must honor the Fathers of the Church, the authoritative teachers through whom we learn the Church's Tradition. The fidelity of some of them cost them their very lives. They died so that we might receive the truth and live, and for this alone we owe them a debt of honor and gratitude. We must also honor the pastors of the Church, including the man who stands at the altar of our own parish, offering the Eucharistic Sacrifice, and speaking the Word of life. "Obey your leaders and submit to them, for they keep watch over your souls as those who will give an account" (Heb. 13:17). There is a reason that the parish priest is called "Father," and as such this fifth word bids us give him his proper honor.

The commandment to honor our fathers and mothers therefore has application beyond the merely domestic. It presupposes a hierarchical world in which everyone is given their due respect due with gratitude.

There are consequences for ignoring this precept, and for refusing to give honor where it is due. Such rebellion eventually introduces a principle of chaos into society, which ultimately reduces one's safety and which forfeits the blessing of God. That is why this is "the first commandment with a promise" (Eph. 6:1–2)—namely the promise that if one honors one's parents one will "live long on the earth." We see the outworking of this promise through our own culture's failure to fulfill it. We are at war with authority in general, and dismissive of parental authority in particular. Our society has replaced the honoring of authority with rebellion against it, which has led to tragic consequences: depression and loneliness too often leading to suicide. Each generation needs the wisdom which previous generations have gained, and the cost of our lack of wisdom has been great. And in the Church, when the priest is not honored as the father of the parish, evil always comes. The fifth word inculcates respect for all authority, and it is out of such respect that stability is born and growth is possible.

Day Nineteen
The Sixth Word (Exod. 20:13)

The sixth word God spoke to Israel on Sinai was:

"You shall not murder."

THIS WORD IS CLEAR ENOUGH, consisting of just two words in the Hebrew: "No murder." It proscribes the deliberate taking of innocent human life. It does not proscribe the killing (or eating) of animals, which was not only allowed, but commanded (e.g., the eating of lamb at Passover), nor does it proscribe the taking of human life in war, which was also commanded. Nor does it proscribe the execution of the murderer, which was commanded numerous times in the Old Testament, and is presupposed in the New (e.g., Matt. 5:21; Rom. 13:4). This word also did not refer to the accidental taking of human life—i.e., manslaughter. If two men fought and one struck another so that he died, but the death was not intended, the guilty party was not to be punished with the same punishment due to someone who deliberately took human life. The one guilty of manslaughter was allowed flee to a city of refuge and remain there until the death of the high priest. But the one guilty of murder was to be executed. (See Num. 35:9ff.) The sixth word deals only with the deliberate taking of innocent human life.

The basis of this prohibition is theological: man is made in the image of God, and so human life is sacred and may not be wantonly taken. That is why the crime of murder is so heinous, and why it is to be punished by taking the life of the murderer. Genesis 9:5–6 says, "From every man's brother I will require the life of man. Whoever sheds man's blood, by man his blood shall be shed, for in the image of God He made man." Capital punishment as the penalty for murder was required by God from mankind (for this precept in Genesis was given to Noah for all men, not to Moses for Israel alone), precisely because all men were made in God's image. Capital punishment therefore does not deny the value of human life, but confirms it. Human life is so valuable that the crime of taking it must be avenged in this way.[1]

It is beneficial to note, as well, that all human life shares the same ultimate value, so that some men are not more valuable than others. The life of the peasant toiling in the fields was as valuable to God as the life of the king sitting on his throne.[2] Human life is therefore not to be valued for its social utility, but for its inherent value to God. God made human life, and He alone is the Lord over life and death. All human life ultimately belongs to Him alone, and He decides who lives and dies. Murder therefore usurps this divine prerogative, as the murderer arrogates to himself the function of dispensing death. This includes self-murder, or suicide—i.e., the active taking of one's own life, whether through violent means or with medical assistance. This is why suicide has been stigmatized by the Christian Church, sometimes to the

---

1   Our Western society is inconsistent in this respect: we devalue human life to the point of multiplying abortions and we also oppose the use of capital punishment as the consequence of murder.

2   It was otherwise in some places and times: some cultures declared that the *weregild* (or "man-price") of a king or a nobleman was higher than that of a peasant, so that the cost of placating or "buying off" the aggrieved family of the deceased was higher or lower depending upon who was murdered.

point of not granting Christian burial to the one who has taken his own life.[1]

Modern society has utterly failed to keep this sixth word. Not only have murders been multiplied in American cities, Islamic terrorism has mushroomed across the globe. In the West, we continue with our state sponsored and funded genocide of the unborn, and now have extended the frontline of our war in the form of euthanasia—in my own Canada euphemistically referred to as "Medical Assistance in Dying."[2] One might imagine that perhaps it consisted of nurses checking your pulse as you lay dying, not actually killing you by lethal injection as was done to criminals on Death Row. Our modern world lives—and dies—in defiance of those two little Hebrew words.

But the sixth word, when we plumb its depths, commands more than that we refrain from murdering our neighbor. For murder begins in the heart with resentment, bitterness, and rage. One thinks of the confession of the repentant murderer in C. S. Lewis' *The Great Divorce*. He confesses the following to someone he knew on earth: "Murdering old Jack wasn't the worst thing I did. That was the work of a moment and I was half mad when I did it. But I murdered you in my heart deliberately, for years. I used to lie awake at nights thinking what I'd do to you if ever I got the chance."[3] We can break the sixth word by murdering our brother in our heart, even if the act is never carried out for fear of apprehension and punishment. Spiritually, though not legally, it is all one: "Anyone who hates his brother is a murderer, and you know that no murderer has eternal life abiding in him" (1 John 3:15).

The Lord Jesus made this clear in His Sermon on the

---

1   Exceptions should be made, such as when the victim was not in his right mind. Pastoral discernment and compassion must be used in making such difficult decisions.

2   Which usually goes by the doubtless unintended, but quite apt acronym "MAD."

3   C. S. Lewis, *The Great Divorce* (Glasgow: Collins Fount Paperbacks, 1984), p. 33.

Mount. The ancients were given the sixth word, "You shall not murder," and anyone who did was liable to the legal penalty of capital punishment in the courts (Matt. 5:21). But the Lord, penetrating to the heart of God's intention of the sixth word, knew that it prohibited murderous rage as well, the silent murdering of our brother in our hearts: "everyone who is angry with his brother shall be guilty before the court" (v. 22). The anger He prohibits with such severity is not mere annoyance, which is unavoidable in human relationships, but the rage and disdain which strips our neighbor of his personhood, which considers him worthless, human garbage—a fit subject for murder, if only we could get away with it. The sixth word therefore does not simply forbid murder; it inculcates love. In murder we sever all possible connection with the one we hate. When we love, we nourish those connections and offer forgiveness. Only by so doing can we fully keep the sixth word.

Day Twenty
The Seventh Word (Exod. 20:14)

The seventh word God spoke to Israel on Sinai was:

"You shall not commit adultery."

A S WITH THE PREVIOUS WORD, this one also consists of two little words in the Hebrew: "No adultery." It prohibits sexual relations with the spouse of another. Sexual relations were only allowed within the confines of marriage. (For Christians, marriage is defined as the union of two adult persons, one male and the other female.) By implication, sexual intercourse was banned in all other circumstances, including premarital sex, cohabitation without formal marriage, and sexual encounters of a married person with someone who is not married.

It is fair to say that such an approach to sexuality is utterly foreign, if not repugnant to modern secular sensibilities, so that modern secular people regard the approach to sexuality in this seventh word with complete incomprehension. To such people these strictures seem perverse. As long as a sexual encounter between adults is fully consensual, what's the problem?

In an earlier time, before the widespread use of contraceptives, one can understand reluctance to engage in widespread and easy promiscuity, since it involved the danger of unwanted pregnancy for the woman. But with the rise of a culture of contraception with its complete severance of sexual intercourse from the possibility of resulting pregnancy, this danger no longer applies in the same way. As long as the appropriate contraceptive measures are taken, people can be as promiscuous as they like. And they ask: what's the problem with this? This commandment prohibiting adultery (and by implication, promiscuity) may have made sense in the Bronze Age Middle East, but it surely has no relevance now. Why is sex banned outside of marriage?

In a word, because God designed sex to serve love, and nothing is more important than love for authentic human living. But first one has to be clear about what "love" means. The word "love" does not refer an emotion or a feeling. Such feelings come and go, and can be produced by raging hormones or strong alcohol, and pleasant as feelings are while they last, they have no moral value.

What can last and what does have moral value is love, defined as a permanent commitment to seek another's highest good, and is not ultimately concerned with feelings of pleasure or pain. Love is an action, and consists of giving the other person what they need, and acting kindly. In marriage, two people promise to love each other forever.

This commitment of love within marriage is by definition permanent. By insisting on life-long fidelity, the Church is not trying to foist unreasonable and arbitrary demands upon married persons which no one could ever keep. When people are in love (that is, when they see each other most clearly), they say the same themselves. Love poetry is filled with promises of eternal constancy.[1] No one writing love poetry

---

1   Even biblical love poetry reads this way. Consider Song of Solomon 8:6–7: "Set me as a seal upon your heart, for love is as strong as death, jealousy as cruel as the grave. Its flames are flashes of fire, a vehement flame. Many waters cannot quench love, neither can the floods drown it. If a man offered for love all the wealth of his house, it would be utterly scorned."

says to his beloved, "I will love you until this feeling wears off," or "I will love you until you get old and wrinkled." Rather, one in love always writes, "I will love you forever, until the stars cease to shine, until the mountains tumble to the sea." Love always binds itself with chains of eternal commitment, and cannot bear the thought of not wearing them.

Sex, with the feeling of closeness that it brings, is meant to express, serve, deepen, and reinforce this love. A lifetime of sex is meant to unite the two lovers ever closer in a mutual bond of commitment, one which will last even after both have grown old and wrinkled, and when the fires of desire have died down. To use sex outside of this commitment is to devalue it and to miss its true purpose. For then sex becomes something not about the other person and your union with and love for that person, but simply about you. Sex becomes merely something that happens inside your own body, a fleeting event for which a relationship or even the presence of another person is not necessary. Human sexuality was designed to be the instrument whereby we could transcend our own desires and to grow—in other words, it was designed to serve relationship and love.

Failure to use sex in this way constitutes a failure to transcend our own desires, with the result that people become simply objects to use. The price for casual sex—or promiscuity, for authentic human sexuality by definition cannot be casual—is an erosion of human personhood. Casual sex involves descending to the level of animals, for sex among animals is never about relationship. When Fido and Mitzi have sex (or "mate" as we usually call it), there is no further significance to the act, apart from the future possibility of puppies. Sex does not establish or serve a higher purpose. Fido feels no need to contact Mitzi after a day or two to see how she is. After mating they go their separate doggie ways, and that's about it.

Casual sex among human beings therefore pushes us in the direction of animals, since it reduces sex to mating. Serial and promiscuous sexual encounters involve severing the sexual act (with its physical release) from any real relationship—especially the relationship of love, which is by definition permanent. Since sexuality is central to human existence and relationships, this failure to rise above animal sexuality is catastrophic for human growth and authentic human living.[1] A life of serial promiscuity short circuits large sections of our true humanity, and makes growth in authentic living impossible.

That is why God designed sex only for love—i.e., for committed human relationship. When confined to such committed relationship, it serves a purpose and produces a result that outlasts the fleeting moments of physical release. Given the age-old (but now all but severed) connection of sex with procreation, one can see that offspring are the symbols of married sexual transcendence. When united to relationship as designed, sex is not just about me and my body, but about something more. It becomes about us, about myself and my spouse. Provided that there are no biological impediments, a lifetime of sex produces children—the tangible expression and result of mutual self-transcendence. For the child is not me, nor my spouse, but something more—the combination of myself and my spouse, the visible fruit of our union and love that will outlast us.

The fact that sex was designed to serve love and not be reduced to the satisfaction of mere bodily appetite is why in the Sermon on the Mount the Lord Jesus said that keeping this commandment involved the inner commitment of the heart, and not simply outward action. A man who looks at a woman to lust after her in his heart—that is, who is inwardly committed an adulterous encounter, and is only prevented from it by fear of being caught—is still guilty of breaking this

---

[1]   That is what St. Paul meant when he wrote that the sexually immoral man sins against his own body—i.e., against the fullness of his potential and life (1 Cor. 6:18).

commandment (Matt. 5:27–28).

The issue here is not sexual temptation (which is inevitable), but commitment: whatever the temptation, the heart that loves and keeps this commandment will remain committed to one's beloved. All human actions find their roots in the human heart, and depend upon what we decide to do when temptation strikes. The purity of heart that God wants is not the absence of temptation, but our commitment to do the right thing even if we could get away with doing the wrong thing.

This seventh word therefore has an abiding relevance beyond that of the Bronze Age Middle East with its restrictive code of sexuality: it offers possibilities for growth for all people everywhere.

Day Twenty-One
The Eighth Word (Exod. 20:15)

The eighth word God spoke to Israel on Sinai was:

"You shall not steal."

ONCE AGAIN and for the third time we find here the same economy of language as was used with the previous two words. In Hebrew this word simply reads: "No stealing."

This prohibition of theft really contains at its heart an exhortation to contentment. Most people who steal today in developed societies do not do so as a means of survival. Most persons committing identity fraud, embezzlement, fraudulent scams, or tax evasion do not perpetrate these crimes because they or their children go to bed hungry and awake each morning to find the table still bare. Nor do most people who shoplift do so because they desperately need what they steal in order to survive.[1] In developed countries, most people who steal commit theft because they want to acquire

---

[1]   We note with sadness the exception of the drug addict who steals to satisfy his addiction. His theft constitutes a special case, since his addiction has compromised his freedom to choose not to steal. The addiction does not justify the theft or relieve the addict from the burden of guilt, but it does make his theft harder to classify with other acts of theft.

more wealth than they can honestly earn, having bought into the lie that the greater the wealth, the greater the happiness.

This is especially so in the affluent West. Our society is driven by the desire to acquire and accumulate, with an entire industry devoted to the art of stoking the fires of our greed—namely, the advertising industry. Our media is awash with images and arguments which both whisper and shout into our ears that we cannot possibly be content or happy unless we acquire whatever item is lately being sold. Human vanity is also enlisted in the service of this consumerism, with some items being priced exorbitantly simply so that most people will not be able to afford them, which makes acquiring them all the more attractive to the few that can. If I can afford a $5,000 purse while others cannot, then having this purse is a sign that I am richer—and therefore better—than others. So, of course I simply have to have one.

The advertisers, of course, know that this is drivel, and so they never actually state plainly, "Buying this will make you happy and contented." The art of advertising consists in its subtlety. One suggests without stating, usually with images and music. But the lying nature of the propaganda can be seen if one steps away from our century and culture to look at previous centuries and other cultures. If it is true the affluence brings happiness and joy, so that the more we possess the happier and joyful we will become, the modern West should be the happiest place on earth. But it is not so.

As an example, in previous times, even in the West, people would sing throughout the day. Men would sing "work songs" as they labored, and women would sing hymns as they baked the family's daily bread. No one sings now, even if music is pumped into our brains through the ubiquitous use of ear-plugs from our mobile phones. We do not ride public transit and see our neighbors singing as they travel to their daily labors, as some people in Africa now sing as they walk to their daily work. On the public transit, most do not even smile.

In fact, rates of depression and suicide in the West are

among the highest in the world. This includes even teen depression and suicide, although arguably no generation has
known such security and affluence as have our own Western
youth. It seems as if the culture of affluence is not only not
a guard against such depression, but is the actual cause of it.
We have demonstrable proof that saying that wealth brings
happiness is a lie.

This eighth word therefore contains the hidden truth that
one does not need to steal to be happy and content, and that
true happiness comes from a relationship with God. The
path of wisdom is to be content with what God's providence
has given us. We do not need to spend our lives scrambling
to acquire, for we will leave everything behind when we die.
As the old proverb reminds us, "There are no pockets in a
shroud." Or, less cryptically, "We have brought nothing into
this world, so we cannot take anything out of it either." All
we need while we live in this world is warm bodies and full
bellies—"If we have food and covering, with these we shall
be content" (1 Tim. 6:7–8). That is all that is necessary; anything else we may receive is by way of bonus.

This contentment is ours by way of decision. We can decide to find our contentment in God alone, recognizing that
"life is more than food" (Matt. 6:25)—that is, life is communion with God. The world will continue to scream, led by
its cheerleading advertisers, that contentment is found at the
end of the road of acquisition. In fact, there is no "way to
contentment" in this life. Contentment itself is the way—we
can decide to find our center and our joy in God, and will
therefore be contented with the daily gifts that He gives us.

Making this decision involves the decision to stop our ears
when the world shouts and tells us to buy more and more. In
other words, we must decide to live counter culturally, recognizing that in the West we live in the midst of a maelstrom
of lies. When the ads beckon to us, we will recognize them as
propaganda aimed at poisoning our minds and stealing our
contentment. It is possibly the best use of the Mute Button—

either metaphorically or literally. We can smile and nod, and refused to be swayed.

This eighth word is aimed at reducing the poisonous fruit of believing the lies of consumerism. A deeper reading of the prohibition of theft will help us not just to avoid the fruit of dishonest and criminal actions, but also the interior roots of that action as well. The flip side of the word, "You shall not steal" is, "You shall rejoice in all that you undertake, in which Yahweh your God has blessed you" (Deut. 12:7). Theft or contentment with joy? The choice remains ours.

Day Twenty-Two
The Ninth Word (Exod. 20:16)

The ninth word God spoke to Israel on Sinai was:

"You shall not bear false witness against your neighbor."

THE ORIGINAL CONTEXT of this word is judicial. When called upon to speak in court to give witness, one must not speak lies—either out of sympathy for the guilty, or because one had been bribed by the guilty. One must look neither to the distressed face of the accused, nor to the riches of the one offering a bribe, but to Yahweh, who sees into the hearts of all men and who is the ultimate Judge of all. One's commitment must be to Him, and therefore to the truth.

This commitment to the truth transcends a merely juridical context. One must speak the truth wherever one finds oneself. In this world, where the father of lies is the god of this age (John 8:44; 2 Cor. 4:4), one can expect to be immersed in lies. And so it is: in the media and in secular culture, one finds oneself swimming in a sea of lies, half-truths, distortions, and insinuations, all of which make recognition of the full truth difficult, if not impossible. Perhaps this is why St. Paul wrote that here [i.e., in this age] we know in part (1 Cor. 13:12). We can only offer that which we possess and thus it is imperative that we acquire the Spirit of Truth.

In this world of lies and half-truths, we can thereby dissipate the darkness and spread the Light of Truth.

The Enemy finds all sorts of ways of suppressing the truth and eroding our truth telling. In first century Palestine among the Pharisees, the strategy was to distinguish between oaths. Some oaths were considered as more binding than others. Thus, if one swore by God's Temple, that oath was not binding, and one could safely swear by the Temple and not fulfill that oath. But if one swore by the gold of the Temple, that oath was indeed binding, and one must fulfill it. Similarly, if one swore by God's altar, that oath was not binding and could be safely set aside. But if one swore by the sacrifice on the altar, that oath was binding, and must be kept (Cf. Matt. 23:16–18).

Christ denounced all such verbal sophistry and casuistry, and insisted simply that a man must keep his promise. He must be so honest that his word was his bond, and that his "yes" meant "yes" so that he could be relied upon to keep his word without the verbal guarantee of an oath. Indeed, he should not swear an oath at all, lest his simple word be put into doubt (Matt. 5:34–37). The confirmation of oaths was unnecessary for a man in whose heart was the Law of God. Such a man would not swear falsely, much less give false witness in court against his neighbor. Such a man would speak the truth at all times, whether under oath or not.

This ninth word therefore inculcates honesty of heart, and a commitment to speak the truth at all times. In this world of lies and half-truths, such a commitment to speaking the full truth of God can be very costly. Sometimes it can cost one's popularity, and even one's livelihood. But the obligation remains. Of course, the truth must always be spoken in humble love (Eph. 4:15), but it must be spoken nonetheless, regardless of the cost. And one may be sure of this: in this age of lies, truth is always spoken at a cost. But faithfulness to Christ demands nothing less. Our Master confessed the truth before Pontius Pilate though it cost Him His very life

(1 Tim. 6:13), and we also must confess the truth before the powers of our age regardless of the cost to us. We may not always (or ever) find ourselves formally in court, but we always walk before the scrutiny and the eye of God. He hears our words, and will reward us for our determination to speak the truth. For all our words are recorded, and will eventually be reproduced before the dread throne of the Lord of glory (Matt. 12:36).

Day Twenty-Three
The Tenth Word (Exod. 20:17)

The tenth word God spoke to Israel on Sinai was:

> "You shall not covet your neighbor's house; you shall
> not covet your neighbor's wife, nor his male slave,
> nor his female slave, nor his donkey, nor anything
> that is your neighbor's."

WITH THIS TENTH AND FINAL word, we go deeper still, leaving the world of outward actions and delving into the depths of the heart, the fountain of such actions. The message of this word is a sign that ultimately the ten words are not simply concerned with external behavior, but internal motivation. Mere laws concern themselves only with what a person actually does in society; the ten words, being the *prolegomenon* (preparatory word) of God's covenant with His people, concern themselves with the human heart which God claims as His own.

The word "covet" does not simply mean "to desire." God does not prohibit desiring, partly because the elimination of desire is hardly possible, being more or less involuntarily. "To covet" means not to desire something in general, but to desire what is owned by another person in particular. As mentioned in the commentary on the first word, if I covet my neighbor's donkey, I do not want a donkey like the one he has; I want his donkey. If I covet my neighbor's slaves, I do not want slaves like the ones he has; I want to take over his staff of slaves. If I covet my neighbor's wife, I want her to leave him and join me. Coveting therefore is the desire to rob another of what they possess, to transfer ownership of the person or thing coveted from others to you.

An illustrative example of coveting is that of King Ahab, found in 1 Kings 21. He coveted the vineyard of his neighbor Naboth, and offered to buy the vineyard from him, or else give him a better vineyard in exchange. Naboth refused the offer, since the vineyard was the ancestral inheritance of his fathers. The king then fell into a sullen depression, consumed as he was with the desire to obtain Naboth's vineyard. Note: Ahab would not be satisfied with a vineyard like that of Naboth; he wanted only Naboth's vineyard. The matter was finally settled (to Ahab's satisfaction anyway) when Ahab's wife, Queen Jezebel, carried out a scheme to falsely accuse Naboth of a capital offense with the successful result that Naboth was unjustly executed. After the vineyard was without owner, Ahab simply moved in and took it. In this case, the sin of coveting led to drastic consequences—the crime of judicial murder.

The roots of the sin of coveting are found in our ungrateful refusal to enjoy and find contentment with the life God gives us. Every day God pours His gifts upon us—beginning with the moment we wake up in the morning, for many people throughout the world die in the night, and do not wake up. He continues to pour gifts upon us, many of which we simply do not recognize as gifts because God provides them for us with such daily faithfulness. The health that we have, the food that we eat, the warmth that keeps us alive, the sight of color, the sound of musical melody, the delicious and fragrant smells we encounter, the feel of loved ones when we hug them or are hugged by them—often are simply taken for granted. We often neither recognize them as heaven-sent from the Father of lights, nor do we thank Him for them.

We might assume that they are somehow simply our due—and are tempted to complain or even blaspheme if we are deprived of them.

The tenth word bids us to be grateful for all God's gifts and to recognize them as such, "paying" for them through the giving of thanks and praise. To each person on earth God gives different gifts. When we fall prey to the sin of coveting, we become blind to the gifts God has given us, and count them as nothing. Instead, we are consumed by a desire for what God has given to someone else. In our folly, we imagine that if only we could obtain what we covet, we would be content, and would never want anything else again.

Covetousness is nonsense, of course, for after despoiling our neighbor of what we have coveted that was his, we soon take this for granted, just as we took for granted all the other good things in our life. We then restlessly move on to covet something else. True contentment, as well as true wisdom and true righteousness, comes only when we turn our eyes away from the blessings our neighbor has and look with gratitude upon the blessings that God has given to us.

And one does this by making a decision and then carrying it out: we decide that our desire to possess what our neighbor has will turn into not coveting what he has by turning our gaze from his life back to ours. The desire to possess what he has may be involuntary, but the sustained attention we give to what our neighbor possesses is not involuntary. It is a choice we make. We can continue to look longingly at what God has given to others, or we can redirect our gaze to what God has given to us. Directing our gaze from our neighbor to our own blessings short circuits the process whereby desiring becomes coveting.

The tenth word was given in terms that the Israelites of that day could best understand. Thus, it spoke of not coveting one's neighbor's house, wife, slaves, or donkey. Today we might add a number of things to that list—including a number of nontangibles. We must also refuse to covet our neighbor's health, talents, marital status, money, position, job, opportunities, success, children, children's success, or worldly recognition. The list could be added to; there is no limit to the number of things we can covet unless we rein in our hearts.

But such reining in remains essential. Only by redirecting our gaze from what providence has given others to the blessings we have received can we truly find contentment, and truly please God. Where the tenth word ends, all real growth in holiness begins. We begin by refusing to covet, and by giving thanks for all that God gives us.

Day Twenty-Four
A Law for Life and Communion

The ten words and the Covenant of God (Exod. 21–23)

IT WOULD BE A SERIOUS MISTAKE to focus upon the ten words as if they constituted the entirety or even the essence of the Sinai covenant. God's purpose in establishing the covenant with Israel was not merely the creation of an ethical people, but a people into whose midst He could dwell. The aim was relationship and communion, not mere morality. Morality and ethical behavior form an essential part of the life of someone in communion with God, but they are clearly subordinate to it, for it is possible for someone to behave ethically and still have no desire for God. An atheist can be ethical. God wanted something more for His people than good behavior: He wanted to be in communion with them so that He could give them life.

The ten words were given directly to Israel from the thunderous summit of Sinai to prepare Israel for a new way of living. Hard as it is for us to imagine today, most religions of the ancient world had very little to do with ethical behavior. Rather, they consisted of keeping taboos and offering sacrifices to the gods—feeding the gods so that the gods would bless them in return. The gods—considered as often dangerously capricious—could give healing, fertility, blessing

upon one's crops and farm animals, and death to one's enemies. They could be (perhaps) persuaded to do these things
if the proper sacrifices were provided in sufficiently generous
amounts, and how one lived one's day-to-day life had little
to do with it.

It was a bit like paying one's bills today: if a man owes
money on his credit card bill, all the credit card people care
about is whether or not the bill is paid. The fact that he got
the money to pay the bill by cheating his friend and robbing
his mother is not their concern. Ancient religion was the
same, and consisted largely of sacrifice and making a deal
with deities; ethical behavior rarely entered into the trans-
action. Israel was often tempted to think like this, and so the
prophets and the psalmist constantly inveighed against such
an idea (e.g., Ps. 50:7ff.).

God therefore began His revelation to Israel on Mount
Sinai by declaring a new and revolutionary way of dealing
with deity. The gods of the nations may not have cared how
their devotees lived, but Yahweh did. His people must strive
to live justly, faithfully, and righteously in their daily lives.
The ten words were not exhaustive, or intended as cover all
the complexities of living an upright life. That is why they
are only ten in number—few enough that a man could count
them on his fingers. Rather than being given as a comprehen-
sive set of regulations, they were examples and pointers at a
new paradigm, illustrations of what God wanted in return
for liberating His people from Egypt. He wanted not just
sacrifice, but their hearts, and the state of their hearts could
be seen by how they lived their lives.

Because the ten words were not intended as a comprehen-
sive system, they were followed by a more detailed set of laws.
Even these were not considered as covering every possible
situation, but were paradigmatic, and capable of application
to other circumstances as well. For example, these other laws
include a provision for making recompense if caught stealing
a sheep or an ox (Exod. 22:1ff.), though one could not claim

immunity from the prescribed penalty for theft because one stole not a sheep or an ox, but a goat. The laws which followed (found in Exod. 21–23) offer a more detailed explanation of how Yahweh wanted His people to live. They presuppose a Bronze Age culture (so that it refers to slaves and the family ox), but enshrines timeless principles of justice, mercy, sexual purity, and a respect for life.

The Covenant Ratified

After Yahweh had given Israel the ten words as the covenant's revolutionary *prolegomenon*, and elaborated on all its legislative details, He invited Israel to ratify the covenant—to "sign on" to living as Yahweh's covenant people. This involved bringing Aaron and his sons, Nadab and Abihu, up to the mountain, along seventy representative elders of the people to worship at a distance, Moses alone remaining close to God. Moses then approached them and recounted for them all the detailed prescriptions (contained in Exod. 21–23) as terms of the covenant, and they agreed to accept them. Actual ratification consisted of a formal recording of the terms of the covenant (here on stone tablets), offering a sacrifice, and sharing a covenant meal.

An altar therefore was built at the foot of the mountain, and sacrifices offered upon it, after which some of the blood of the sacrifices was sprinkled upon the people assembled below. Moses, Aaron, Nadab, Abihu, and the seventy elders then ascended the mountain to eat the sacrificial meal with Yahweh, sealing the covenant. At this meal they saw the glory of Yahweh, and "under His feet there appeared to be a pavement of sapphire, as clear as the sky itself" (Exod. 24:10). Despite seeing the glory of Yahweh, He "did not stretch out His hand against the nobles of the sons of Israel; they saw God, and they ate and drank" (v. 11). Israel was now no longer a group of slaves benefiting from Yahweh's kindness, with no one allowed to approach Him under any circumstances whatever. Now they were His covenant people, for their elders had been invited to eat at His table. In the culture of the Near East, after such a shared meal they were now bound to each other by bonds of covenant loyalty.

A Tabernacle for Communion

After the Covenant had been ratified, God again summoned Moses to the top of Mount Sinai. The Covenant was established so that Israel could have communion with God dwelling in their midst, and all ancient people knew that communion with the gods was made possible by sacrifice. Accordingly, Moses ascended the mountain one more time, remaining there over the next forty days to receive stone tablets containing the ten words (as a symbol of the entire covenant),[1] and the instructions regarding how Israel was to offer sacrifices to Yahweh. These instructions included all the details about how the Tabernacle and its altars were to be constructed, set up, and function, and how the priests were to offer sacrifices upon the altars. Compared to shrines found in other parts of the ancient Near East, the Israelite arrangement is primitive and simple—as one might expect from a nomadic people then in the desert. It was designed to be portable, unlike the immovable shrines and temples of the Canaanites, or the stationary locations such as holy springs, hills, or trees. Israel had been established as an army on the move, a pilgrim people, constantly open to the guidance and leading of their God, and a portable shrine befit their nomadic condition.

Once the shrine was set up and the priesthood consecrated and functioning, Israel could safely come and approach

---

1   Cf. Deut. 4:13. Writing tablets in that day were small enough to be held in one hand. Two tablets were used, the second a copy of the first. According to the practice of that day, two copies of covenants or treaties were always made, one for each of the two parties to the covenant or treaty.

the holy God, communing with Him, and finding blessing and joy in His presence. This was the goal of the shrine: that the consuming fire which set the summit of Sinai ablaze could dwell in the midst of His people, and that, like the burning bush, they would not be consumed. Rather, they could come into His courts with praise where their heart and flesh could sing for joy to the living God (Ps. 84:2).

— *Lessons from the Lawgiver's Life*

The divine choice to dwell in a humble and portable shrine (rather than in an elaborate and immovable temple), with the advantage of Christian hindsight, reveals something about God and His expectation for us.

First of all, it reveals the humility of God. Perhaps the series of small curtains and tents (the outward court measured only one hundred and fifty feet long by seventy wide; the Tabernacle itself measured forty-five by fifteen feet) was all that a recently liberated group of slaves could manage to construct in the wilderness. But even after Israel had long been settled in the land and had access to more wealth and artistic splendor, God gave no instructions for a more elaborate structure.

In fact, when David, possibly embarrassed at the primitive simplicity of the shrine compared to the more splendid buildings he was planning on erecting for his own palace, told his prophet-advisor Nathan that he was planning on building God a more elaborate temple, he received a rebuke: "Are you the one who should build Me a house to dwell in? For I have not dwelt in a house since the day I brought up the sons of Israel from Egypt even to this day, but I have been moving about in a tent, even in a tabernacle.[1] Wherever I have gone with all the sons of Israel, did I speak a word with

---

1   The Hebrew word is *mishkan*, a temporary shelter, like a shepherd's tent.

one of the tribes of Israel, saying, 'Why have you not built
Me a house of cedar?'" (2 Sam. 7:5–7). The primitive simplicity of the shrine was part of the divine intention, not a
mere concession to the circumstances of the time. It wit-
nessed to the divine humility.

It was this humility which would later allow the One who
dwelt in the humble tents of nomads to dwell in the womb of
an unknown young Jewish girl from Nazareth, and then later
to grow up and learn the trade of a carpenter, living for thirty
years in working class obscurity, and then finally dying upon
a cross, betrayed and rejected by His own people. The humility of the Messiah might have become an insurmountable
stumbling block if God had not already manifested Himself
in humility to the Hebrews. In hindsight we can discern the
divine humility that would result in the Incarnation in the
humble construction of the wilderness shrine.

Secondly, the portable nature of the shrine reveals what
God expected from His people—namely a willingness to
move with Him, to follow His lead, and to journey to new
places. Pagan religions all had something timeless and un-
changing about them. They did not develop and evolve, so
much as survive. It was otherwise with the God of Israel. He
had come to lead His people on a journey.

It was a long journey, beginning at Ur of the Chaldeans,
when God called Abraham to travel to a new and undisclosed
place, and to live his entire life as a wanderer. It continued
with a journey into Egypt, then out of Egypt, and then into
the Promised Land of Canaan. The fact that the shrine was
portable and was moved to several locations within Canaan
revealed the nomadic journey God intended for His people.
They were to regard themselves as forever a people on the
move, willing to journey and change.

That journey would eventually bring great changes indeed,
as Israel was at length called upon to be transformed as the
New Israel, the Church—transcending all ethnicities, tribes,
colors, and languages. Like Abraham the wanderer, the Israel

reborn had no final homeland here in this age, but was to seek the city which has foundations, whose maker and builder is God (Heb. 11:10). The changes which Jesus brought to His people should have come as no surprise to those who knew the hidden meaning of the portable shrine.[1]

---

1   This was the main point of the speech Stephen made in his defense before the Sanhedrin in Acts 7.

Day Twenty-Five
Apostasy at Sinai: Worshiping the Golden Bull

Apostasy

ISRAEL'S FAITHFULNESS to the covenant into which they had just entered vanished soon enough. Moses had not told Israel how long he would be gone, and when days turned into weeks and he did not return, they concluded that perhaps something had happened to him, or that he had abandoned them. They therefore turned to Aaron, his brother and coleader since their days in Egypt. They "assembled about him" (Exod. 32:1), threatening and demanding that he take over the lead, since Moses was obviously not returning. With the end of Moses there also came the end of his absurd insistence on not having images representing Yahweh. Of course Yahweh must have an image! How else could anyone worship Him? In their fear of having been abandoned, they insisted upon a return to familiar ways.

Aaron therefore, perhaps also perplexed at his brother's unexpectedly long absence, reluctantly agreed. An image must be found—Yahweh was strong, the source of life, fertility, strength. A young full grown bull [in Hebrew '*egel*) would serve as His image very well, and was consistent with the Egyptian thinking that they were used to. Aaron collected the gold from the earrings donated for the purpose by their wives and children and melted it down to provide gold plating for a wooden statue of the young bull.

When he introduced the final product to the waiting Israelites, he attempted to link their (non-Mosaic) future with their immediate (Mosaic) past: "These are your gods,[1] O Israel, that brought you up out of the land of Egypt!" In Aaron's later recounting of the story to Moses, the rebellious mob had demanded, "Make gods for us!" accustomed as they were to the polytheism of Egypt.[2]

Here Aaron was perhaps attempting to preserve at least some of the worship of Yahweh—perhaps even by creating only a single image of Yahweh as a young bull, rather than many images of the requested many gods. As is often the case with such compromises, it utterly failed. The image was to be consecrated and made functional at a feast the next day, which Aaron called, "a feast to Yahweh," in another attempt to preserve continuity. The image and feast were a great success with the people, who embraced the old familiar ways with enthusiasm. There were sacrifices, sacrificial meals, music, and dancing. The revelry became louder and louder, and began to get out of hand.[3]

We are meant to detect a note of irony in Aaron's proclamation of the dedication ceremonies for the new image as "a feast to Yahweh." It was anything but a feast to Yahweh, but was a great sin against Him, a repudiation of Moses and of all that Yahweh had done through Moses—including the gift of

---

1   In Hebrew *elohim*; here a true plural, since a plural verb is used with it ("who brought you up").

2   Some scholars suggest that the plural refers to the Canaanite practice of worshiping the same god at different locations as different gods, so that the plural refers to different shrines of the same god. But Israel's experience up to that time was Egyptian, not Canaanite.

3   The text does not explicitly say that sexual excesses accompanied the revelry, but it was not unlikely. The word used in Exod. 32:6 and often rendered, "The people sat down to eat and drink and rose up to play" is the Hebrew word *tsahaq*, which has an explicitly sexual meaning in Gen. 26:8.

water from the rock and the (still continuing!) daily gift of manna. It was pure syncretistic idolatry, a blatant violation of the ten words they heard at the foot of Sinai and which they had solemnly promised to obey. Like many pagan feasts, it began to degenerate into immoral chaos. The worry and fear that had gripped them at the thought of Moses leaving them (either because he had died on Mount Sinai or because he had abandoned them and gone elsewhere) now gave way to a time of relief, expressed in celebration and uproarious feasting. The intensity of their revelry indicated how anxious and fearful they had become during Moses' long and unexpected absence.

Judgment

After God had given Moses all the instructions needed for establishing the shrine, He told Moses to go down quickly back to his people, for they had apostatized already, and were in the middle of an idolatrous time of feasting before their idol. Such a spectacular act of apostasy from the covenant they had just ratified called for swift judgment. Yahweh therefore declared that, given that Israel was irredeemably inclined to rebellion and apostasy (as Israel abundantly demonstrated even before they reached Sinai), He would wipe them out for their crime and start over, making a great nation out of Moses' descendants instead.

Moses' concern was for God's glory. He entreated God to relent and argued that if Yahweh did wipe them out here in the wilderness, it would only give the Egyptians the opportunity to blaspheme against Him. They would say, "See? Yahweh knew that He couldn't give the Promised Land to the Hebrews, and so He destroyed them in the wilderness to cover it up!" He implored Yahweh to remember not the faithlessness of Israel, but the faithfulness of the patriarchs, and to spare His people for the sake of Abraham, Isaac, and Jacob. In mercy God allowed Moses' intercession for Israel to prevail.

But Moses' intercession for Israel did not mean he minimized their sin. When he came to the foot of the mountain and saw the spectacle for himself, he threw down the stone tablets, the symbols of the covenant that God had given him to carry back to Israel, shattering them on the ground. It was not just an impulsive act of anger, but a prophetic act to show them the significance of what they had done. They had imagined that they remained faithful to Yahweh, and that the changes made in Moses' absence were simply legitimate ritual tweaks made to make the covenant more familiar. Moses knew that the changes represented a repudiation of the covenant, a flagrant violation of the second word inscribed on the stone tablets, and an act of idolatry.

He took the gold plated wooden image of the young bull and burned it, grinding the gold plate to powder and throwing the ashes and the ground up gold plate into the Israelites' water supply, making them drink water that their sin had thus tainted. This action too was not a vindictive act of anger, but a way of letting Israel know the magnitude of they what they had done: with every mouthful of water, they would taste the result of their sin.

He also rounded on his older brother Aaron, and demanded to know how he had let himself be party to this outrage. Aaron knew he was without excuse, and humbled himself, calling Moses, "my lord" even though Moses was his younger brother. In his pathetic retelling of the story, he obliged the people, throwing their gold into the fire when—lo and behold!—out came that bull!

Meanwhile, the people were getting ever more out of the control. He therefore called aloud for help: "Whoever is for Yahweh [i.e., whoever opposes this outrage]—to me!" Immediately members of his own tribe of Levi came to support him. Moses then spoke as a prophet of the Lord: "Thus says Yahweh, God of Israel: Every man put his sword on his thigh and go through the camp and kill every man his brother." In other words, find those who refused to repent of their idolatry and execute them as idolaters. They did so and a number were killed.[1]

The concept of executing someone for apostasy is foreign to our modern way of thinking, but that is because we live in a liberal democracy, and one with a separation of church and state. It was otherwise in the ancient world, where it was felt that unpunished blasphemy of the gods would result in divine retribution to everyone in society. In Israel especially, such blasphemy could not be allowed to go unpunished, since Israel was a theocratic state in covenant with Yahweh. In that world it was understood and accepted that enticing neighbors to commit apostasy was a capital offense. Moses' actions in purging the unrepentant idolaters from Israel were in keeping with the thought of this time.

— *Lessons from the Lawgiver's Life*

Describing the Israelites' actions at the foot of Mount Sinai as "apostasy" is an interpretation, based on the view of religion found in the ten words and the Law of Moses generally. It was not intended as and did not feel like apostasy to the Israelites worshiping and dancing about the golden bull. In the same way, the religious practices of later Israelites which combined the worship of Yahweh with the worship of Baal and the other gods of Canaan were not intended by them as acts of apostasy either. They considered it to be simply broadminded, a generous acceptance and incorporation of the religious practices of their neighbors.

Those pagan religious practices, like the religious practices of Israel, had long and venerable histories, and had given

---

1   A comparatively small number: if the total population of consisted of over two million, then the stated number of the slain as "three thousand" was but a small fraction. Perhaps the "three thousand" here should be read as "three companies or families," consisting of perhaps 30 people. See comments in the footnote on Exod. 12:37 in chapter nine above.

comfort and solace to those who practiced them for generations, if not centuries. Who were the Israelites to reject
them and say that they were wrong? The ancient syncretism
of Israel, whether practiced at the foot of Mount Sinai or in
the land of Canaan, was viewed by them as a kind of cosmo-
politan ecumenism, a live-and-let-live acceptance of all the
religions in the world. If asked, no doubt they would have
said that all the various paths and religions were true, or that
at least they seemed to "work" for those who practiced them.
But Israel was wrong, and Moses was right. The other religions were forbidden to Israel because they involved not communion with the true and saving God, but with the demons.
And many of their practices, such as sacred prostitution and
child sacrifice, were abominable. At the foot of Sinai, Israel
was not being broadminded, but faithless.

This provides a cautionary tale for us today, when so many
religions exist in the modern marketplace. The religious
shelves are full of products—not just the well known ones
like Christianity, Judaism, (and now) Islam, but varieties of
Buddhism, Taoism, religions indigenous to North America
(sometimes called "Native spirituality"), and a multitude of
self-actualizing options recently grouped together in a single
basket called "New Age." Like the many religious options
available in Moses' time and later, most of them share a spirit of broadmindedness,[1] and assert that though their option
is of course the best, all paths lead to God. This conviction
is so pervasive today that it scarcely needs stating, and the
religions which deny it come in for fair bit of criticism and
pillorying in the public press.

Nonetheless, for those willing to learn from the Lawgiver's life, it remains true that all paths do not lead to God, and
that, for Christians, Christianity is true and leads to God in
a way that other faiths do not. This does not mean that only
Christians will be finally saved, and that all non-Christians

1   Islam being a notable exception.

will go to hell. It does mean that what the Gentiles sacrifice, they sacrifice to demons, and not to God (1 Cor. 10:20). God can of course accept and save whoever He wills in His mercy.[1]

We must therefore remember that what tries to pass itself off as broadminded ecumenism, can often be simple apostasy. In baptism we Christians have been joined in a covenant to God, just as the Israelites were, though our covenant is a new one, made in the blood of Christ. Our duty consists of faithfulness. We must remain true to what we have promised to God, and not violate the covenant we have made.

[1] But if a non-Christian is saved, he or she is not saved because of their religion, but in spite of it.

Day Twenty-Six
Restoration at Sinai: Renewing the Covenant

Moses' Intercession

DESPITE MOSES' ANGER at Israel's apostasy, he still had a heart for his people, and he once more trudged up Mount Sinai to intercede for them. God had promised that He would not destroy them as they deserved, but their final punishment had yet to be decided. At the summit of Sinai Moses pleaded with God to forgive His people, and not to blot them out of His book—i.e., the book containing the names of His favored ones.[1] If anyone had to fall from His favor, Moses pleaded that it be him! "Let me," Moses cried, "take the place of the idolatrous sinners!" The request revealed as nothing else could Moses' greatness of heart.

---

[1]   Kings in those days kept a register of those whom they favored, those who could expect special treatment from the king; see Esther 6:1–2 and Mal. 3:16. This book served as a metaphor for those whom God favored. Until Israel sinned, they could expect favors from God, such as being led safely into the Promised Land, but now they had forfeited this favored status. Moses offered to forfeit his own favored status if theirs could be retained. One should not read into this text the later New Testament use of the image as the record of those having eternal life in the Kingdom of God (e.g., Rev. 3:5).

Nonetheless, the request was denied: "Whoever has sinned against Me," God replied, "him I will blot out of My book." God did, however, agree to lead Israel to the Promised Land. But He would not go with them Himself, nor dwell in their midst, as He had intended and as the instructions for shrine and priesthood had provided. That had all been forfeited by their sin. And mercifully so—"I will not go up in your midst, for you are a stiffnecked people, and I might destroy you on the way" (Exod. 33:3). It was clear that Israel's sin might well provoke yet more punishment, with the final result that they would be destroyed. God would no longer go with them as they traveled, nor dwell among them in the promised shrine with its Holy of Holies. He would, however, send His angel to lead them to Canaan (Exod. 32:34; 33:2).

News of this calamity brought great sorrow and mourning to the people when Moses descended the mountain to give them the news. Moses erected a tent a good distance outside the sinful camp of the Israelites to meet with God. It was there that God would speak with Moses face to face, as a man speaks with his friend and equal. And it was there that Moses once again pleaded with God to reconsider and withdraw His punishment from Israel.

"See," he pleaded, "You say to me, 'Bring up this people to Canaan!' But You Yourself have not let me know whom You will send with me." By "sending someone to be with" Moses, Moses meant that God had not revealed who would be with him to give protection. Merely being led to Canaan by an angel was not enough; Israel needed God Himself to be with them. How, Moses asked, could Israel find forgiveness for their sin so that God would reconsider and go with them—both on their journey to Canaan and dwelling among them in the Tabernacle shrine as first intended?[1] At this, God re-

---

1   Or, in the words of v. 13, "Let me know Your ways that I may know You, so that I may find favor in Your sight." The "ways" refer to how Moses can change His mind and find favor in His sight so that He reconsiders.

lented, and said, "My presence shall go with you."

Wanting to make sure this was a firm promise, Moses continued, "If Your presence does not go with us, do not lead us up from here." The promise, however, was firm: "I will also do this thing of which you have spoken, for you have found favor in My sight." Moses had succeeded! God would now go with them to Canaan as planned, and would allow the shrine to be built with the functioning priesthood and sacrifices so that He could dwell in their midst and they could approach Him.

Then Moses added another bold request: "I ask You, show me Your glory!" One may ask: Why did Moses want God to show him His glory? The context and the results of the theophany strongly suggest that it had less to do with Moses' personal desire to behold God and more to do with the success of his mission as leader of Israel. Beholding God's glory would add tremendously to his authority—an authority which they constantly challenged before their arrival at Sinai, and which they had utterly repudiated during his forty-day absence on Mount Sinai. Moses was motivated not by a desire for mystical experience, but by a desire to obtain the credibility with his people that he needed to lead them.

God granted this bold request, and promised that after he left the Tent of Meeting and ascended to the top of Mount Sinai, He would make all His goodness pass before him and would "proclaim the name of Yahweh" before him (Exod. 33:19)—i.e., He would grant a theophany which would reveal how He would deal with Israel ever after. One's name revealed one's character, and Yahweh's name contained His character and power. When Yahweh "proclaimed His name," He was thereby revealing how Israel would experience that character and power—namely as sovereign in grace and compassion: "I will be gracious to whom I will be gracious, and will show compassion on whom I will show compassion." Yet despite this revelation of Yahweh's character and power, Yahweh would not reveal His face, for no one could see His face and live, or endure the full blast of His glorious presence.[1] Moses therefore would only experience the fading afterglow of His presence. Yahweh would have Moses stand in the crevice of a rock on Sinai's height and Yahweh would cover him over until He passed by. Moses would only see His "back"— i.e., His fading glory when He was departing.

In preparation for this, Moses should therefore ascend to the summit of Sinai again, this time bringing two tablets of stone like the ones which he had broken. As at the initial encounter when God gave the ten words, care must be taken that no one transgress the set boundaries and approach the mountain.

Theophany of God's Goodness and Glory

Moses obeyed, and the next morning ascended Mount Sinai with the two blank tablets of stone in his hands. As promised, Yahweh descended in a cloud before him as Moses called upon Him to manifest His glory. He revealed His glorious goodness, proclaiming His name: "Yahweh! Yahweh God! Compassionate and gracious, slow to anger and abounding in covenant-loyalty[2] and faithfulness, who keeps covenant-loyalty for thousands, who forgives iniquity, transgression and sin, yet will no means leave the guilty unpunished!" This proclamation effectively promised that Yahweh would indeed honor His promise to forgive the sin of apostasy with the golden bull, and restore all that Israel had recently lost. No wonder Moses made haste to prostrate himself in gratitude to God.

Encouraged by Yahweh's assurance of His forgiving nature, one last time Moses asked Him to renew the covenant

---

1   One is reminded of the Orthodox distinction between God's essence and His energies; no one can see God in His fullness as He is (His "essence"), but can truly experience His presence through His "energies," i.e., His actions toward us in this world.

2   Hebrew *hesed*.

and to dwell in their midst. God responded by indeed renewing the covenant, and restating again what He required of Israel. As a sign of this covenant, Yahweh again wrote the ten words upon the tablets Moses had brought with him.

The reason Moses requested this vision of God's goodness and glory was to add to his credibility among the people. God had now restored His covenant to Israel; Moses also needed a restoration of his authority as God's representative if he was to fulfill his own role in that covenant. And such was the power of God's presence that even the afterglow of His glory left its mark upon Moses. Perhaps Moses had planned on relating to Israel the authenticating theophany of God's glory which he had seen. He found when he arrived back at the camp that words were not necessary: "the skin of his face shone because of Yahweh's speaking with him" (Exod. 34:29). So powerful was the sight that even Aaron, along with all the sons of Israel, were afraid to come near him.

This was quite the change: before, Moses was simply "the man who brought us up from the land of Egypt" (Exod. 32:1), whom they assumed had somehow abandoned them and whom they quickly repudiated. Now, his authority was such than none dared approach him. He insisted that they draw near, and "commanded them to do everything that Yahweh had spoken to them on Mount Sinai" (Exod. 34:32)—no more rejecting the word of Yahweh or contemplating apostasy! Out of compassion for them, after this Moses put a veil over his face whenever he moved among the children of Israel and spoke with them. When he went into the tent of meeting to speak with God, of course, he removed the veil.[1] Once again, Moses' love for his people and his boldness before Yahweh had rescued Israel from the fruit of their own apostasy and sin.

---

1   See St. Paul's application of this to the Jewish unbelief of his day in 2 Cor. 3:12–18.

— Lessons from the Lawgiver's Life

This passage reveals, as perhaps does nothing else in the Old Testament, the patience and loving-kindness of Yahweh. Far from being the severe, arbitrary, judgmental, unforgiving, and warlike deity that heretics like Marcion[1] later imagined Him to be, Yahweh was indeed a God who was compassionate and gracious, slow to anger and abounding in covenant-loyalty and faithfulness, who keeps covenant-loyalty for thousands, who forgives iniquity, transgression and sin. Israel had committed a terrible sin against Him, sealing many prior sins of rebellious grumbling and ingratitude in one final act of idolatrous apostasy—and that immediately after receiving the ten words and ratifying the covenant, solemnly promising to obey all that Yahweh had commanded. The total destruction of the people and their replacement with the descendants of Moses would have been entirely justified.

Yet simply because Moses interceded for them and pleaded with God to forgive them, reverse His decision, and completely reinstate them to their former dignity and status, God did so. This shows that He is a God who delights to forgive, and who does not desire the death of the sinner, but instead yearns for the sinner's repentance that he may live.

Such boundless compassion, patience, and love would find final expression in Christ. While we were yet sinners and rebels, Christ died for us (Rom. 5:8). Given that the heart of God burns with love for all that He has made, and despite the tragic fact that much of His creation has turned against Him in implacable hostility, it is hardly surprising that in Christ He accepts sinners, prostitutes, and tax collectors, i.e., people notorious for their lack of a moral compass. He desires the salvation of all, so that everyone may return to God without fear, no matter how grievously they have sinned and

---

1   A heretic in the second century who denounced the deity of the Old Testament as utterly unlike the God of the New Testament and denied that they were the same God.

rejected His Law and His love. At the heart of the Gospel is the open and bleeding heart of God.

This passage also reveals that the final goal of our salvation is glorification—or, in more technical terms, *theosis*. That is, God's goal for us is that we become by grace all that God is by nature. By nature, God is immortal, sovereign over nature, overflowing with joy, peace, and love. By His grace we are to share these qualities, thus becoming "partakers of the divine nature" (2 Pet. 1:4). In Biblical terms, we are to share God's glory.

Moses saw God's glory on Sinai's summit, and became a partaker of that glory. Beholding the glory of God, he became glorious himself, and shone with divine splendor to such a degree that he had to veil his face when walking among his brethren. This is what happens when we are exposed in faith to the glory of God. When we see Him just as He is, we become like Him (1 John 3:2), and even in this life, as we behold the Lord, we are changed from glory to glory (2 Cor. 3:18). This was God's predestined goal for those whom He foreknew would believe in Him: to be conformed to the image of His Son, so that Christ becomes the firstborn of many brethren (Rom. 8:29). Those whom God foreknew would believe, He glorified (Rom. 8:30), so that they would share the very glory of Christ. On Mount Sinai, Moses became a prophet of *theosis*.

Day Twenty-Seven
The Presumption of Nadab and Abihu

A S ISRAEL CONTINUED to dwell at the foot of Sinai, after having received Moses' instructions for the building of the Tabernacle and all that the priesthood needed to function, and began to build according to divine command, they received further instructions about those sacrifices. These were contained in our Book of Leviticus. This book contains a further example of Israel's rebellion—that of Aaron's sons Nadab and Abihu.

The privilege of ministering at the newly-built shrine belonged to Aaron and his four sons. One part of their priestly ministry consisted of the daily offering of incense. Every morning and every evening, incense was to be burned upon the altar of incense which stood in the Holy Place, just outside the curtain separating the Holy Place from the Holy of Holies, wherein rested the Ark. They were not to offer unauthorized or "foreign incense," gathered from anywhere and consisting of any ingredients, but only the incense especially made for the purpose and consisting of the ingredients God has specified (Exod. 30:9; 34–38).

One day, two of Aaron's sons, Nadab and Abihu, "offered foreign fire [i.e., unauthorized incense] before Yahweh." The judgment was severe and immediate: "fire came out from the presence of Yahweh and consumed them, and they died before Yahweh." So quickly did the judgment come that they were still in their priestly vestments when the fire consumed them, not having had time to change. Their corpses were dragged outside the camp, since dead bodies would bring ritual uncleanness to the holy shrine wherein they fell.

Because they were slain for their sin, Aaron and his remaining two sons were forbidden to make the customary wailing and mourning for them, lest it seemed that they did not deserve the judgment and that Aaron thought that Yahweh was to blame for their deaths. Moses' reaction was summed up in a couplet recorded in Leviticus 10:3, "It is what Yahweh said: 'I must be sanctified among those who are near Me, and I must be honored in the presence of all the people.'" In other words, as those with responsibility for drawing near to Yahweh as His priests, Nadab and Abihu should have known better. They had only themselves to blame.

What was the nature of their sin? The text of Leviticus does not say. Given the reference in Exod. 30:9 to "foreign incense," it is possible that their offense of offering "foreign fire" consisted of disregarding Yahweh's command to offer only incense made to the divine specifications. And given the command which was given after recounting that Nabab and Abihu died after offering foreign incense that the priests should "not drink wine or strong drink...so that you will not die" (Lev. 10:9), it seems likely that Nadab and Abihu died because they became drunk and offered incense upon the altar of incense that Yahweh had not authorized in their drunken state. Whatever the particulars of the offense and its punishment, their sin reflected adversely upon Moses and his brother Aaron.

Some modern readers have opined that the judgment of Yahweh upon Nadab and Abihu was unjustly harsh, and far in excess of their actual offense. After all, what was the problem with offering the wrong kind of incense, or in some other way not keeping the liturgical rules? Surely such a small mistake did not deserve such severe punishment! Such a view reveals the gap that exists between the ancient understanding of worship and the place that "rules" play in it, and our modern understanding, with its almost total disregard for and misunderstanding of holiness.

For moderns, the concept of holiness is primarily ethical, and it describes a life of virtue. For the ancients, holiness was almost entirely liturgical, and it described the power of the deity one was approaching—and consequently the danger of approaching the deity wrongly. In our modern understanding, anyone should always have free access to anyone else, even to God. Thus, in our view, anyone can freely approach God at any time.

The ancients assumed the opposite, and believed that only God (or the gods) had the right to authorize who could approach Him (or them) and under what circumstances. The details which authorized that approach were therefore crucial. Ignoring those details and approaching God in defiance of them constituted the sin of presumption. Rules mattered, because keeping them showed God that one approached Him in humility. Nadab and Abihu were not slain merely because the ingredients of the incense they offered were not those specified by Yahweh, so much as because they arrogantly presumed to dispense with Yahweh's rules and set their own.

All the ancients would have understood this, and would not have been surprised that the presumption of Nadab and Abihu resulted in their deaths. The lesson they would have drawn from it was not how mean and unreasonable Yahweh was, but how holy He was—which of course is why the story was recorded in Leviticus in the first place. The severity of the judgment revealed the holiness and the greatness of Yahweh—and therefore how powerful He could be in dealing with Israel's many foes and in defending His covenant people.

— Lessons from the Lawgiver's Life

What therefore can we learn from the terrible experience of Nadab and Abihu—apart from the obvious lesson that one should not serve in the temple of God while drunk? Heeding the original ancient lesson of the story, I suggest that the experience of Nadab and Abihu also teaches us that God must be served and worshiped as He commanded, and not according to our own whims and ideas. We might imagine that we have the right to worship God in any way we like, so that the worship of God becomes an opportunity for human self-expression and creativity. All that matters in worship, we might say, is whether or not our worship is sincere. As long as our worship expresses what is in our hearts, it is authentic, legitimate, and pleasing to God.

The fire which consumed Nadab and Abihu proved that this not so. In worship, God looks not so much for our creativity as for our obedience. Infractions of this principle no longer result in death, but it remains that God has revealed how He wants His Christian people to worship Him.

This notion has sometimes been called "the regulative principle of worship"—i.e., the conviction that God reveals how He should be worshiped, and that His people should conform to what He has revealed. In the Church, this means that the principles and patterns which the apostles delivered to the churches abide as perennial paradigms for how the Church should worship God. In particular, the basic pattern of Scripture reading, instruction based upon that reading, intercessory prayer, the exchange of the kiss of peace, the Eucharistic prayer commemorating Christ's sacrifice as an introduction to the corporate receiving of bread and wine as His Body and Blood, abides as the perennial pattern for Sunday worship ever after.

In other words, the apostles left the Church not only teaching about who Christ is and how His people should live, but also how His people should worship Him in their Sunday *ekklesia*, or gathering. They did not leave them to their own liturgical devices about how to worship God any more than they did about what to believe about Him or how to live so as to please Him. Rather, they left them a *regula,* a rule, a pattern, so that they might tell the coming generations in turn how Christians should live.

The alternative to such specific guidance was to leave the Church to its own devices—i.e., without the leading and direction of the Holy Spirit. When the Lord promised that He would send His Spirit who would lead His disciples into all truth (John 16:13), this truth included such details as to how to worship Him. This guidance was not provided through the subjective feelings of individual Christians, but through the authoritative direction of the apostles. The churches did not have to guess what the Lord wanted them to do when they assembled together on the Lord's Day. The apostles gave them these directions when they were with them and they provided an example of what they were to do after they had left.

Divine worship therefore is not a matter of us expressing our own feelings to God, but of following the pattern and direction that Christ left us through the example of the apostles. Substituting our own ideas, feelings, and the expressions of our hearts for what the apostles have left us is not acceptable this is offering "foreign fire" in defiance of the express directions and examples which the apostles have left us. The result may not be the fire of judgment which consumes the leaders (or perhaps the "praise band"), but it will still not be what God had intended for His people.

Divine blessing comes when we obey the pattern and directions which God has left us—either through Moses or through the apostles—and if we do not follow that pattern, we forfeit the blessing which God wants to give us. The form of the Christians' Sunday worship is important. It can be the instrument through which God gives us His sacramental divine blessing, or merely the expression of our loving thoughts and good intentions. It all depends upon whether we obey God's apostolic direction or offer foreign fire to God.

Part Three

THE WILDERNESS
WANDERING

Day Twenty-Eight
Judgment in the Wilderness

The Sin of Israel

AFTER SPENDING ALMOST A YEAR at Mount Sinai and nearly fourteen months after their departure from Egypt, eventually Israel set off for the Promised Land. Moses convinced his brother-in-law[1] Hobab to accompany them so that Hobab, who knew the Sinai Peninsula well, could act as their scout and guide: "We are setting out for the place of which Yahweh said, 'I will give it to you'; come with us, and we will do you good, for Yahweh has promised good to Israel'" (Num. 10:29). The request reveals the optimism and confidence which Moses had in their imminent possession of the Promised Land more than it does his need of a guide. His optimism was also apparent from the cry he uttered whenever the camp would set out: "Arise, O Yahweh, and let your enemies be scattered, and let them that hate You

---

1   The Hebrew is *hoten*, sometimes (confusedly) rendered "father-in-law." The term means "relation by marriage," and thus can indicate either one. The issue of the respective identities of Reuel, Jethro, and Hobab has been much debated. Reuel is never called Moses' *hoten*. I suggest that Reuel was leader of the clan, Jethro was Moses' father-in-law, and Hobab was his brother-in-law. See also footnotes for chapter 2.

flee from before Your face!" (v. 35). After so many months of waiting, apostasy and restoration, and building, they were finally on their way! Moses' confidence in Yahweh is record-ed in contrast to Israel's pessimism and rebellion, which are recorded in the following chapters.

Taberah

The story of their journey begins by saying that "the people became like those who complain of evil in the hearing of Yah-weh" (Num. 11:1). Note: not just "the people complained," but "the people became like those who complain"—i.e., they changed into a group of chronic complainers. After all the patience that Yahweh had shown them in the face of their rebellion and apostasy, still they complained! That was why "when Yahweh heard, His anger burned and the fire of Yah-weh burned among them and consumed some of the out-skirts of the camp." The fire refers to lightning strikes (com-pare 1 Kings 18:38; 2 Kings 1:10). The judgment could have been worse: it consumed only the perimeter of the camp, and did not fall within the more heavily populated center of the camp itself. Indeed, the Hebrew word *qatseh* (sometimes rendered "outskirts") can indicate a place on the outer bor-der outside the camp, where those who were unclean had to stay until they were ritually clean. Thus, the fire did not fall within the safety of the camp itself.

What was the source of the complaint? We are not told, since the point of the story is that Israel was becoming trans-formed into a company of rebellious complainers, and not the specific complaint itself. In the subsequent record of complaints, the text specifies the ostensible reasons for those complaints—namely, that the people lacked meat (11:4), that Moses had married a Cushite woman (12:1), and that Moses was unduly exalting himself (12:2). Here the reason for their gripe is left unspecified. But since this story follows on a series of stories recording the preparations to leave Sinai

(Num. 10), including the note of how long they had been encamped at Sinai (10:11), the complaint here might have centered upon how long they had been stuck at Sinai. In Egypt, Moses had promised them plenty and abundance in the Promised Land of Canaan, and here they were stuck in the desert, far from plenty or abundance. They were impatient to get what they were promised, and complained that Yahweh had not kept His promise—maybe because He was not able to give them the Land as He had promised to do? Such an insult against Yahweh's power would be reason enough for the angry demonstration of His power.

After the fire of God struck the perimeter of their camp, Israel believed again in His power, and feared further judgment. They cried to Moses to intercede for them, and God hearkened to Moses' cry, so that the fire abated. They called the place of the strike "taberah,"[1] which meant "burning," to remember the danger from which they were delivered.

Kibroth-hattaavah

Yet the complaints continued. The next one had in source in "the rabble who were among them"—i.e., the non-Israelites who had left Egypt along with the Israelites (Exod. 12:38). Their rebellious talk spread to the Israelites themselves, who were now fertile ground to receive any such murmuring. The Israelites had lived in Goshen, the breadbasket of Egypt, and they remembered the varied diet there—now made more desirous and delicious in their memory since they were sustained in the wilderness primarily by the manna. They spoke incessantly of the cucumbers, melons, leeks, onions, and garlic—all conspicuously absent from their desert tables, since these vegetables required much irrigation—and began to

---

1   The site is not mentioned in the list of campsites in Numbers 33, so that the burning probably took place in the area of their next campsite at Kibroth-hattaavah.

despise God's miraculous supply of bread. Each family stood wailing at the entrance of their tent, which given their large numbers would have made a great deal of noise. It was as if the entire camp was bewailing a death.

Not only was Yahweh angry at this continual complaining and ingratitude, but Moses was distressed also. Given Moses' previous pastoral concern for his people and his willingness to be punished in their stead if that were the only way for them to find mercy, one can imagine how the spectacle of everyone weeping would have affected him. His anger and resentment at having to bear the burden of caring for them alone was rooted in his love for them.

In frustration he lashed out and cried to God, "Why have You been so hard on Your servant? Are these my own children that I should be burdened with caring for them all like a nurse carries a nursing infant? Where am I to find enough meat to give such a large crowd? They are too much for one person! If this is how it must be, then just kill me now!"

Yahweh answered Moses' prayer, both in providing help for him in leading them and in giving them meat, and the solution for both problems involved God's *ruach* (see notes on the Hebrew word *ruach* in chapter 10). First, Yahweh told Moses to gather seventy elders from the people whom age had taught wisdom[1] so that He would place upon them the same *ruach* or spirit that He that had given to Moses. These men would share with Moses the burden of leadership. Secondly, there went forth a *ruach* from Yahweh, and this wind brought quails from the sea into the camp. They flew low to the ground, about three feet above the ground,[2] so that they could be snared in great numbers. These would provide the meat they craved—and not just for a day, but they would

---

1   Literally, "Seventy men from the elders of Israel, whom you know to be the elders of the people" (Num. 11:16).

2   It is possible that the reference to the height of three feet refers to the height of the piles of the quails gathered.

catch so many quails that they would be eating their meat for an entire month, until they were sick of it.[1]

God's *ruach* thus brought an unmixed blessing to Moses, but a mixed blessing to Israel. Indeed, more than simply giving Israel so much meat that the sight of it sickened them after a while, it became a judgment upon them as well. Since they had despised Yahweh and His provision of manna in the wilderness, a plague struck them as they ate their first taste of quail, and many died immediately after eating it. A doctor today would recognize the plague as widespread food poisoning, caused by Israel not taking care to preserve the quail meat properly. Whatever the medical cause, Israel was learning that making a choice based on rejecting God's provision always leads to death. After the judgment struck, the place was named "Kibroth-hattaavah" in memory of the disaster: "Graves of Greed."

— *Lessons from the Lawgiver's Life*

The humanity of Moses shines through in his frustration at having to bear the burden of care for all his people, especially when it involved being subjected to the sound of their sorrowful lamentation and pain. His humility shines through when God responds to his frustration, and provides help for him. From these things we learn two important lessons about true leadership.

The first lesson concerns the necessity of divine provision for true leadership. God delegated the task of finding suitable helpers to Moses himself, so that the leaders would be men of proven character and wisdom. But mere proven character and leadership are not enough for the task of lead-

---

1   Literally "Until it comes out your nostrils and becomes loathsome to you" (Num. 11:20). The LXX reads, "and becomes nausea to you"—in Greek "χολέραν (*choleran*) to you" (compare the English "cholera"!). The text says that each person gathered at least ten homers—i.e., thirty-eight bushels.

ing the people of God. These men therefore joined Moses at the Tent of Meeting where God routinely met with Moses, and there God placed upon these men the same Spirit that He had placed upon Moses so that they might share his qualifications for leadership. Human talent alone is insufficient. Guiding the people of God requires that the leader be endowed with the Spirit of God.

The second lesson concerns the importance of humility for true leadership. Moses might have thought that all the seventy men who were chosen were present with him at the Tent of Meeting, but two were still in the camp at the time when God poured His Spirit upon the elders who had been chosen. This was apparent, because when the Spirit rested upon the men, two of the chosen men, Eldad and Medad, prophesied while in the camp—i.e., spoke ecstatically and loudly[1]—thus alarming those around them. When news of the scandal reached Moses along with a request that he restrain them, Moses refused to do so. Instead, he commented, "Are you jealous for my sake? Would that all Yahweh's people were prophets, and that He would put His Spirit upon them!" Far from being threatened that others shared his gifts and authority in the camp, Moses rejoiced in it. He was not jealous of his own position, but only wanted the work of Yahweh to be done. Such self-forgetful humility is the hallmark of a true leader.

---

1   The Hebrew word "to prophesy" can also mean "to rave"—compare its use in both 1 Sam. 10:10 and 1 Kings 18:29, where the verb is usually translated "prophesied" and "raved" respectively. Prophetic behavior in the Old Testament could be so ecstatic as to be almost involuntary—see 1 Sam. 19:19–24.

Day Twenty-Nine
Judgment in the Wilderness

The Sin of Aaron and Miriam

AFTER THEIR DEPARTURE from Kibroth-hattaavah, Israel arrived in Hazeroth, where Moses faced yet another challenge—this time from within his own family, where he could have expected unqualified support. His older sister Miriam and his older brother Aaron confronted him about the choice of his second wife[1] because she was a Cushite woman—i.e., a woman of Nubia (i.e. Ethiopia), a country which also had been oppressed by Egypt. If she was a woman from among the "mixed multitude" of Exod. 12:38 that left Egypt and which was the source of the latest complaints that led to the disaster at Kibroth-hattaavah (Num. 11:4), such resentment is at least explicable. Look at what happens when we trust these non-Israelite foreigners! And you married one of them!

The complaint about Moses' choice of wife masked a deeper grievance. Miriam and Aaron felt that their young-

---

1   Some suggest that the reference was to Zipporah, but this seems unlikely. The identification of her here as "a Cushite woman" indicates that she is being introduced for the first time. Also, if the objection were to Zipporah, why did they wait for so long to bring it up?

er brother was unduly exalting himself over them. After all, Aaron functioned as Moses' mouthpiece before Pharaoh in Egypt, and Miriam (who helped her baby brother find a home with the Egyptians) also shared that authority as a prophetess herself (Exod. 15:20). It seems that the confrontation over Moses' wife soon escalated so that they lashed out with their real concern, demanding, "Has Yahweh spoken only to Moses? Has He not spoken to us as well?" That is, they felt that Moses was claiming an exclusive role in leadership that was not his, and it was in this prideful spirit that he imagined he could marry a foreign woman over the objections of his older siblings. (It is possible as well that they felt resentful at not being chosen to be among the seventy Moses picked to receive a share of the Spirit and his authority in Israel.)

Miriam took the lead in confronting Moses, since her name is listed before Aaron's, and the divine judgment upon their challenge, when it came, fell solely upon her. Aaron may have simply allowed himself to strongarmed by her as he allowed himself to be similarly strongarmed by the people when they demanded a golden bull-calf. Moses was hurt by such an attack coming from his own brother and sister, and no reply of his is recorded. An explanatory note is provided which says that "Moses was very humble, more than any man who was on the face of the earth" (Num, 12:3). That is why he said nothing in his own defense. But, ominously, the text relates that when Miriam and Aaron ganged up on him like this, "Yahweh heard it" (v. 2).

And Yahweh's response was immediate. He summoned all three of them "suddenly" (v. 4) to the door of the Tent of Meeting and then descended in the pillar of cloud. He was not about to let such a challenge to Moses pass unanswered. He demanded that Miriam and Aaron come forward, and emphatically declared that Moses' authority was unlike that of anyone else. Yahweh might speak His word to a prophet in visions or dreams, but Moses was different. To Moses

Yahweh spoke "face to face," as a man might speak to his colleague, without the mediation of vision or dream. "Why then," Yahweh demanded, "were you not afraid to speak against My servant Moses?"

It was an angry and rhetorical question, and Yahweh did not wait for an answer. After saying this, "His anger burned against them and He departed" as the cloud of His presence withdrew. But after He had gone, Miriam was left leprous, as white as snow.[1] Miriam's leprosy was not what we today call "leprosy" (i.e., Hansen's Disease), but an extreme form of psoriasis or eczema, leucoderma, or shingles. Aaron looked at her in horror, and immediately appealed to Moses to plead with Yahweh for her healing. It represented a tremendous *volte face* on his part: Aaron, with Miriam, had just insisted that Moses had no greater authority with God then they did, and now they were relying upon just such an authority to affect a healing. Moses, ever humble, immediately cried out to Yahweh to heal his sister.

Yahweh granted Moses' prayer. But anyone who had contracted such a skin disease would still have to remain in isolation outside the camp for a week before being pronounced clean (thus Lev. 13). Miriam must bear a like punishment and acknowledge that she had unjustly dishonored Moses by her challenge. If she had dishonored her own father who reacted to her dishonor by spitting in her face, she would not dare to appear in public for seven days (v. 14). Let her remain in public isolation for the prescribed week, as a sign of her repentance for dishonoring Moses. But even here punishment was tempered with mercy. God did not move the people to the next campsite until after the days of Miriam's isolation outside the camp were finished, but waited for her as a sign of the esteem which she had justly earned until then.

---

1   One wonders in passing if there was some irony intended in this: they complained that Moses had married a Nubian whose skin was darker than theirs, and now Miriam is afflicted with skin that was too white.

— *Lessons from the Lawgiver's Life*

In these events we see the divine reward for humility. Moses must have been deeply hurt when challenges and criticism arose from within his own family. Family solidarity in that culture demanded that his siblings honor him and support his leadership, especially when it had proven so effective and had received the obvious approval of God. God had spoken to him and chosen him to lead Israel out of Egypt to the Promised Land, and Aaron was only included in that leadership role because of Moses' initial reluctance to accept the divine call. Miriam had no leadership or prophetic role whatsoever, and was only honored as a prophetess because she was the sister of Moses and Aaron who functioned as prophets.[1] As Moses faced challenge after challenge to his authority from the rebellious Israelites, he must have taken solace from the support he received from his family. Yet even his own brother and sister were turning against him, and joining those who challenged his authority.

As well as being personally hurtful, such a challenge was also politically dangerous. The challenges from the people were sufficiently intense that Moses feared once that they might stone him as a prelude to choosing another leader and returning to Egypt. This undercurrent of discontent might easily boil up again if the people felt that even Moses' own brother and sister sided with them against him.

Yet what could he do? The issue was not who was most important among them, but rather who Yahweh had chosen to have unique and supreme authority to lead Israel. The question could be argued, but could not be decided by argument alone. Besides, such was his humility (and probably his hurt in the face of an attack from his own family) that he was not inclined to defend himself. Here was a classic case of the folly of self-assertion. "Let another praise you, and not your

---

1   Thus Exod. 15:20 refers to her as "Miriam the prophetess, Aaron's sister." See the relevant footnote in chapter 10.

own mouth, a stranger, and not our own lips" (Prov. 27:2). Like the Lord Jesus before Pilate, as a lamb before its shearers is silent, so Moses did not open his mouth. He uttered no threats, but kept entrusting himself to Him who judges righteously (Isa. 53:7).

The immediate response from the righteous Judge offers an encouragement to all who suffer hurtful and unjust accusation. Rarely has humility been so quickly rewarded, or such innocence been spectacularly vindicated. In this age, those who suffer unjustly and are falsely accused must usually have to wait for the Last Day for their vindication and for the sentence of the just Judge. That is why waiting in silence is so difficult in this age, and why humility is so rare.

But it remains the path we must tread, nonetheless. To assume the mantle of leadership will inevitably involve receiving unjust criticism and cruel slander. We may be tempted to respond by opening our mouths and praising ourselves, and even uttering threats. It is true that sometimes speaking in our self-defence is required, and that challenging unjust accusations may become necessary. Even the Lord Jesus at His interrogation before Annas challenged those who slapped Him unjustly (John 18:23). But we cannot control the actions of others, and effective and godly leadership will inevitably excite envy and opposition. We cannot forever be defending ourselves. Like Moses at Hazeroth and the Lord Jesus before His accusers, we must be prepared to leave our final vindication with God.

Day Thirty
The Mission of the Spies

AT LENGTH ISRAEL CAME to Kadesh Barnea, in the wilderness of Paran, the desert in the northeast part of the Sinai Peninsula. That is, they were almost at the border of Canaan, which then included all of modern Palestine, Lebanon, and much of southern Syria. Israel's time of slavery and their long trek through the desert lay behind them. In front of them lay the land of Canaan, and it was now time for them to enjoy what Moses had promised them in Egypt: a land flowing with milk and honey, a land wherein they could find rest. The final triumphant chapter of their story was about to begin! They were almost home.

As a preparation for their invasion and conquest of the Promised Land, Moses sent out spies, a man chosen from each of the twelve tribes. They were to head north as far as Lebo-hamath, north of Damascus, a distance of about 250 miles. In their travels they were to find out such details as would be needed for the imminent military operations—such things as the populations, whether the land could support them while they invaded and fought, whether the towns were unfortified camps or walled cities. They were also instructed to bring back some of the fruit of land—probably for the purpose of encouraging Israel to invade and take possession of the land that could produce such fruit. The narrative adds the note that this last instruction was given because "it was the time for the first ripe grapes"—i.e., late summer or early fall (Num. 13:20).

When the spies returned forty days later after fulfilling their mission, their report was not what Moses had been expecting. They began by reporting, "We went into the land where you sent us"—a significant and ominous beginning of their report, since all previous references to the land had called it "the land which Yahweh swore to give them" (e.g., Numb. 13:2; 14:16). The spies omitted this part of the description of the land. They acknowledged that it was indeed a land that flowed with milk and honey, but they went on to insist that there was no way they could conquer it. The cities were large and fortified, and the giant descendants of Anak lived them, and men so large that the spies were like mere grasshoppers in comparison. The land devoured its inhabitants, and it would surely devour them if they invaded. The project was impossible.

Their report had its intended effect, and the people lifted up their voices and wept at the catastrophe. They had come so far and endured so much—all for nothing! One of the spies, Caleb by name, tried to hush the peoples' wailing, and offered a minority report, encouraging them to trust Yahweh, who would indeed give them the land as He swore to them that He would, but the people refused to listen. Caleb's words were shouted down by the other spies and drowned out in the general din.

Then they turned on Moses and Aaron, who they blamed for their catastrophe and for convincing them to undertake such a stupid and hopeless project, and for subjecting them to such suffering in the wilderness for so long. It would have been better to die in the wilderness, or even back in Egypt, than for them to invade such a land and be killed there and have their wives and children taken as slaves by the victorious Canaanites! Enough of this madness! Let us appoint another leader, and follow him back to Egypt. Fearing for their lives, Moses and Aaron fell on their faces before the roaring assembly of rebellious Israel. Caleb and Moses' aide Joshua tore their garments in grief and mourning at hearing such a plan. They pleaded with them not to do this, but to continue to trust Yahweh. He would give Israel victory—only let Israel not rebel against Him now by renouncing His plan for them at the very moment when victory was at hand! But Israel would have none of it, and were ready to stone Moses, Aaron, and all their supporters with stones as a prelude to returning to Egypt.

It was then, at the moment of crisis, that the glory of Yahweh appeared at the Tent of Meeting, and He was furious. "How long will this people spurn Me?" He asked Moses, "and how long will they not believe in Me, despite all the signs which I have done in their midst?" Yahweh was ready to consume them all and start over again, making the descendants of Moses into a great nation in Israel's place.

Once again, despite the fact that Israel was about to stone him to death, Moses interceded for them, and tried to convince Yahweh not to destroy Israel as they deserved. He repeated the argument he had used before, and even quoted Yahweh's own words back to Him, reminding Him that He had promised to be "slow to anger and abounding in covenant-loyalty, forgiving iniquity and transgression" (see Exod. 34:6).

And once more Yahweh relented and hearkened to Moses' intercession. He would not destroy Israel immediately and start over, but their sin would not go unpunished. Israel had refused to obey God and enter the Promised Land? So be it: they would not enter the land, but would die in the wilderness, which they themselves had said was preferable. Let them head back toward the wilderness by the way of the Red Sea. As many days as the spies had been away, disobediently looking on the land of Canaan with fear, that many years would Israel wander in the wilderness. The spies had said that if they invaded Canaan, their children would become slaves there? Very well: it would be those very children who would enter and take Canaan as conquerors, after their rebellious parents had died in the wilderness. The exception would be Caleb and Joshua, who remained faithful and obedient. They would survive the period of wilderness wandering, and would inherit the Promised Land. The spies themselves would face a more immediate judgment, and would die by disease.

The supernatural presence of the glory of Yahweh was enough to convince the people of their folly in heeding the spies' report—but not enough to bring them to obedience. They mourned this latest sentence, which condemned them to spend the rest of their lives in the wilderness of Sinai. The next morning, they had yet another plan: they had changed their minds, and now would indeed go up to invade and conquer the land of Canaan! They were motivated not by true repentance, or a desire to now obey Yahweh, but by a horror of the thought of remaining in the wilderness all their lives. Moses pleaded with them not to invade the land in defiance of Yahweh's orders and in the absence of His promise to be with them. The spies were correct that the Canaanites were mighty: victory was only certain because Yahweh would be in Israel's midst. If He were not in their midst, there was no way Israel could win. But once again, the hearts of that generation were hard. They refused to listen to Moses, and proceeded to invade—with the inevitable results. The Canaanites north of them struck them and scattered them as far as Hormah.[1] The name "Hormah" was fitting, as it was the Hebrew word for "destruction."

— *Lessons from the Lawgiver's Life*

The report of the spies and the resultant debacle that followed form one of the great and tragic hinges of Israel's history. Israel was poised to enter the Promised Land and com-

---

1   The precise location is disputed; some place it east of Beer-sheba in Palestine's far south.

plete their long trek from Egypt through Sinai when it all fell apart, dooming that generation to forty years of pointless wandering. What might have been the prelude to a new day turned to the twilight of a long night. This fiasco offers us three lessons.

First, it teaches that in the tasks we have been given by God we must keep our eyes not on the attending difficulties, but on the Lord who set us the task. Success or failure often depend upon where we fasten our focus. Focusing upon difficulties or potential difficulties is certain to produce failure. God, who gives us strength for the tasks He sets, can also give us victory and crown our efforts with success. When problems arise like giants in the land, we must say with Caleb, "We should certainly arise and take possession, for we shall surely overcome" (Num. 13:30).

Secondly, when difficulties arise, we must refuse to allow bitterness, cynicism, or fear to rule our hearts. Despite the threat to his life from his fellow Israelites, Moses still prayed for them, and interceded that they might not be destroyed. This urgent intercession, coming as it did in a moment of crisis, revealed as nothing else had his greatness of heart and nobility of spirit. His heart was committed to his people, and had been since his youth when he sided with them in Egypt. Despite Israel's constant doubting him, rejecting him, opposing him, and now threatening to kill him, he continued to love them. In this also Moses foreshadowed the Lord Jesus: "In return for my love, they act as my accusers; even as I make prayer for them" (Ps. 109:4).

Finally, the example of the Israelites reveals that everything depends upon obedience. When God told Israel to believe in Him and go up to conquer the land, they should have obeyed, but they did not. And then later, when He told them not to go up and conquer, but to turn back to the wilderness by way of the Red Sea, they still disobeyed. The issue was not conquering the land, but obeying the Lord. If He told them to wander in the wilderness, they could not be blessed for obedience in Canaan.

It all hinges upon obedience. Here one thinks of the Narnian story of The Silver Chair, as written by C. S. Lewis. The Christ-figure Aslan gave the children Jill and Scrubb orders to obey, one of which was to find a lost prince. They would recognize him by this sign: he would be the first person they met who would ask them to do something in the name of Aslan. When they met an apparently dangerous lunatic tied to a chair, he demanded that they untie him in the name of Aslan. Could this lunatic be the lost prince? Wasn't it too dangerous to untie him? Scrubb wondered aloud whether "everything will come right if we do untie him." The answer came back: "I don't know about that. You see, Aslan didn't tell Jill what would happen. He only told her what to do. That fellow will be the death of us once he's up, I shouldn't wonder. But that doesn't let us off following the sign."[1]

This was the attitude Yahweh required of His people at Kadesh Barnea. Whether our actions result in life or death, all that matters is that we obey God and do what He has told us.

---

1   C.S. Lewis, *The Silver Chair*, chapt. 11 (p. 626 in *The Complete Chronicles of Narnia,* HarperCollins, 1998)..

Day Thirty-One
The Rebellion of Korah and the Budding Staff

The Rebellious Coalition

IT IS NOT CLEAR FROM THE SCRIPTURES when the next challenge to Moses and Aaron's authority came. The absence of precise dating is probably significant, since it reveals the rebellious spirit that animated Israel throughout the time of their forty years of their wilderness wandering.

That rebellious spirit had been percolating in many forms within the people, and it coalesced in a single confrontation, as the Levitical family of Korah joined with Dathan and Abiram from the tribe of Reuben in opposing the hegemony of Moses and Aaron.[1] Each group had different complaints. What united them was their opposition to the program of Moses, in which Moses led the people of Israel as undisputed leader and Aaron and his family constituted the priesthood which alone was entitled to offer sacrifice to Yahweh.

The Levitical clan of Korah objected to the priesthood being confined to the family of Aaron, and those from the tribe of Reuben (Reuben being the firstborn of Israel) seems

---

1   Numbers 16:1 also mentions On the son of Peleth, sons of Reuben, as joining their rebellion, but nothing further is said about them. Perhaps they withdrew early from the anti-Mosaic coalition.

to have objected to the tribe of Levi (the tribe of Moses and Aaron) being given special privileges within Israel. Since Reuben was Jacob's firstborn, they doubtless felt that if any tribe should have been given special privilege, it should have been theirs. These Levites and these Reubenites made common cause in hope of toppling Moses from his leadership. Korah gathered 250 supporters, men who were important and influential among the tribes of Israel and confronted him, challenging his authority to lead the people.

Their argument was that all of Israel was holy to Yahweh (which was true), and that therefore Moses was wrong in claiming authority over them (which was not true). They were not arguing that no group should be entrusted with the priesthood or that anyone might serve as a priest, but that the priesthood should not be confined to the family of Aaron. They argued that the priesthood should be open to all the tribe of Levi—i.e., to themselves. For Moses and Aaron to insist on confining it to the family of Aaron constituted exalting themselves above the entire assembly of Yahweh. Anyone from the tribe of Levi should be able to offer sacrifice to Yahweh at his Tent of Meeting shrine.

Obviously, the choice of who had priestly access to Yahweh belonged to Yahweh alone, and so Moses proposed that all the 250 men who claimed they could offer sacrifice to Yahweh try to do so. Let them appear before Yahweh tomorrow to offer the morning incense, and let Yahweh Himself decide. Korah and his clan should have been satisfied with the privileges Yahweh allowed them as Levites and not coveted the access allowed only to priests. Their resentment and sin were not against Moses and Aaron, but ultimately against Yahweh, for the decision to confine the priesthood to the family of Aaron was not Moses' or Aaron's decision, but Yahweh's.

Then Moses asked that Dathan and Abiram to come to meet him, presumably to enlist their support. They refused to comply, lest it appear that by answering Moses' summons they were subordinate to him. Who was Moses to lord it over them? They would not come up to meet with him at the Tent of Meeting! Moses was the one who brought them up from the land of milk and honey—i.e., from Egypt!—to die in this barren wilderness.

It was an extraordinary thing to say. In their view, Moses had promised them a land of milk and honey, but Sinai was clearly no such thing. Compared to Sinai, Egypt was a land of milk and honey, and the fields and vineyards he had promised them were far away. Moses was obviously deceiving the people[1] with his promises of Canaanite fields and vineyards, and so could not be trusted. Moses was indignant at this accusation, and protested to God that far from lording it over Israel and enriching himself at their expense, he had not taken so much as a single donkey from them.

The contest would begin tomorrow. Let the supporters of Korah present themselves at the Tent of Meeting to offer their incense, and Yahweh would decide who He accepted as priests with access to Him. That morning, Yahweh appeared in glory and wrath at the Tent of Meeting, and would have consumed the rebels in an instant if not for the intercession of Moses and Aaron. The contest therefore began, and two hundred and fifty challengers began to offer the morning incense.

God was also angry at the rebels of the tribe of Reuben who remained at their tents. Moses warned everyone to back away from their tents, lest they perish in the judgment that was about to overtake them. Moses spoke to all the people who had gathered there. "By this you will know," he shouted, "that Yahweh has sent me—if these men die a normal death, then Yahweh has not sent me. But if Yahweh brings about something new and the earth opens up and swallows them alive, then you will know that in opposing me you have rebelled against Yahweh!" And sure enough, the earth opened

---

1   Literally, "boring out the eyes" of the people, and blinding them to the truth.

up and swallowed them alive, consuming the tents of rebellion occupied by the conspirators Korah, Dathan, and Abiram. They and their families went down alive to Sheol, in an unprecedented judgment of their rebellion. The 250 allied with Korah fared no better: when they offered their incense to Yahweh, fire went forth from Him and consumed them for daring to offer strange fire to God, and for rejecting the privileged priesthood of Aaron.

The Plague

One would think that such a judgment would have settled the matter once and for all. Remarkably, it was not so. The next morning, all the people blamed Moses and Aaron for the deaths of Korah and his supporters and for the deaths of the families of Dathan and Abiram. Once more, Yahweh was angry at such perversity, and was prepared to consume Israel instantly; therefore, a plague of judgment broke out among the people, and they began to die.

It was a moment of crisis and emergency, for the plague threated to consume the entire people. Moses told Aaron to quickly take a censer, fill it with burning incense from the altar, and run among the people, offering sacrifice for their sin to make atonement for them. Aaron therefore ran in the middle of the crowd with his incense, and in response to this sacrificial intercession, the plague ceased where Aaron stood, so that his position among the people marked the boundary between the living and the dead. It was a clear revelation that only the priesthood and intercession of Aaron were acceptable to God, and that his priesthood alone could atone for sin and avert divine judgment. Without Aaron's priestly ministry, Israel could not hope to be spared. The only way they could live and not die now that the holy God dwelt in the midst of His sinful people was if Aaron offered the sacrifices for them.

The Final Proof

There was, however, a third and final confirmation of God's choice of the house of Aaron to be His priests. Yahweh spoke to Moses and required that each of the heads of the twelve tribes submit their staff[1] to him after carving the name of their tribe upon their staff. Another staff, the staff of the tribe of Levi, would be added, with the name "Aaron" carved upon it. These would all be placed before God in the Holy of Holies, and God Himself would choose which staff or tribe He wanted to minister to Him.

They did so, and the next day they found that the staff of Aaron, which was in the middle of all the other staffs, had sprouted and put forth buds, beautiful white blossoms, and ripe almonds. Though it was a staff of dead wood like all the other staffs, yet it proved to be alive, to the point where it could produce fruit. The miracle proved that the house of Aaron alone had been chosen by God to give life to Israel. The sign had its desired effect, and Israel knew that Aaron and his sons had been divinely chosen to approach God. All others who attempted to draw near as priests would perish.

— *Lessons from the Lawgiver's Life*

The rebellion of Korah, Dathan, and Abiram reveals the importance of abiding by the restrictions which God sets regarding how we are to approach and worship Him. The temptation to enviously covet the office of others and to therefore ignore the restrictions which God has imposed is a perennial one. We see this temptation functioning in the modern debate over whether or not women may serve God as presbyters and bishops in the Church.

The apostolic tradition is clear that God has restricted the pastoral office to men—and to certain kinds of men—

---

1   In Hebrew the same word, *matteh*, is used to mean both "tribe" and "staff."

men who are not new converts, and who have only been married once (1 Tim. 3:1ff.). As St. John Chrysostom said about those entrusted with directing the church, "Not only must the entire female sex step back from so great a task, but also the majority of males."[1] The historical teaching of the Church is clear: women may not be ordained priests or presbyters or bishops.

Many today regard this two-millennia-old restriction of the Church regarding its pastoral offices as possessing no contemporary relevance or weight, and they discard the Church's past restrictions as quickly and emphatically as Korah and company discarded restrictions insisted upon by Moses. Such modern advocates of the ordination of women insist that such restrictions are unfair and arbitrary, that these restrictions deny the essential worth of women, and deprive the people of God of the gifts they have to offer. Their arguments therefore are identical to those put forward Korah, Dathan, and Abiram—and so possess no more legitimacy than those of Korah, Dathan, and Abiram. What matters in worship is not the recognition of perceived human rights, but our humble submission and conformity to revealed will of God. God does not look for the gifts we have to offer, but for our obedience. Self-will that is set in defiance to what God has established can never substitute for such obedience.

---

1   St. John Chrysostom, *Six Books on the Priesthood*, trans. and intro. Graham Neville, Popular Patristics Series 1 (Crestwood, N.Y.: St. Vladimir's Seminary Press, 1977), p. 20.

Day Thirty-Two
Grumbling at Kadesh: Water from the Rock

AFTER THE DEATH OF MIRIAM, in the fortieth year of Israel's wandering, when the generation who had made their exodus with Moses was nearing their end, they came once again to Kadesh, near the border of their entry into Canaan. And once again, as thirst consumed the Israelites and threatened to destroy them with their cattle,[1] they rebelled against the leadership of Moses and Aaron, even as they had for the last forty years. They said to them, "If only we had died when our brothers died before Yahweh!" This reference was probably to the last time the leadership of Moses and Aaron had been effectively challenged by Korath, Dathan, and Abiram. Once again rebellious Israel rehearsed the unfulfilled promises of Moses and Aaron: they had promised to bring them to "a place of grain or figs or vines or pomegranates" (Num. 20:5), but here there was not even water to drink, and they were about to die! Moses and Aaron were obviously liars, who did not speak for God!

Again, Moses and Aaron prostrated themselves before Yahweh at the doorway of the shrine, asking for help and direction. The direction came soon enough. Moses was to take

---

1   Perhaps there had been an unexpected drought in the area; otherwise one wonders why Moses would have brought Israel back into an area that was known to have no water supply.

the staff of Aaron which had budded, and which lay before Yahweh in the Holy of Holies, and stand before the entire assembly next to a prominent rock. In their hearing, he was to speak to the rock and command that it yield water. Then, miraculously, without any further action from Moses, the rock would gush forth water and satisfy the thirsty people, thus proving once and for all Yahweh's power to help and save them.

Moses, however, after forty years of provocation, rejection, and rebellion, had had enough. He took the challenge to Yahweh's authority personally, and regarded it as a challenge to his own authority, which he felt needed bolstering. At that moment, he felt the crisis was about him and his honor, not about the honor and power of God. He allowed his long suppressed anger at his people to boil over, and he used the direction God had given him to bolster his own status before the people. It was now all about Moses!

"Listen now, you rebels!" he shouted, addressing Israel in an angry way that he never did before. "Shall we bring forth water for you from this rock?" His wording is significant. By "we" Moses meant "Aaron and I," whose personal authority he felt was being challenged, not the authority of Yahweh. Accordingly, instead of obeying Yahweh and simply speaking to the rock to vindicate Yahweh's authority, Moses struck the rock twice to vindicate his own. The repeated striking of the rock was an expression of anger, intended to demonstrate to all how futile it was to challenge Moses' authority over the people of Israel.

In mercy God still made water gush forth from the rock to satisfy His thirsty people, but Moses had still committed a great sin. His job as Yahweh's servant had always been to vindicate Yahweh's authority over Israel. Moses was simply God's instrument, God's servant, and his authority had been given him for the sole purpose of glorifying Yahweh—not to glorify himself. Moses' frustration and anger, long pent up over a generation's worth of rejection,[1] had pushed him into glorifying himself and using Yahweh's power to solidify his own power base and security within Israel.

Yahweh's response was immediate: "Because you have not believed in Me so sanctify Me before the sons of Israel, therefore you shall not bring this assembly into the land which I have given them." By his egotistic and angry choice to use God's power to exalt himself in Israel rather than God, Moses had forfeited the gift of leading Israel into the Promised Land. That task would now lay with another. This judicial sentence—a mere eighteen words in Hebrew—are among the saddest words in the entire Bible. Having come so far and having endured so much, Moses was now forbidden to enter the Promised Land with his people. The waters that gushed from the rock at Kadesh were the waters of Meribah, or "the waters of argument," for after forty years Moses found himself at Meribah all over again. Israel had not yet learned the lesson of trusting Yahweh even after the passage of forty years, and now even Moses was caught up their rebellion. In a diatribe lambasting Israel, Moses had called them "rebels"— and God would later accuse him of the very same sin (Num. 27:14).[2]

The passing of this rebellious generation was illustrated by the reference to the death of Aaron when Israel journeyed onward from Kadesh and reached Mount Hor.[3] Aaron's death before entering the Promised Land is connected to

---

1   Perhaps grief over the recent death of his sister also contributed to his fall.

2   The same Hebrew word [*marah*] is used in both Moses' denunciation of the Hebrews in Num. 20:10 and Yahweh's condemnation of Moses in 27:14.

3   The location is uncertain. Some suggest that the site cannot be the traditional site of Jebel Nebi Harun near Petra, for this was within Edom and not near its border as the text says in Num. 20:23, and they suggest as a more likely candidate Jebel Madurah, about fifteen miles northeast of Kadesh. Others accept the traditional location, noting that the borders of Edom were shifting.

Moses' rebellion at Kadesh, for Aaron had obviously been complicit in Moses' decision to use Yahweh's power to exalt their authority and status in Israel.[1]

His high priestly authority devolved upon his son Eleazar, a sign of God's mercy to Israel—Aaron might die, but the priesthood of Aaron's house and God's presence among Israel would continue. By bookending the story of Moses' rebellion and its punishment with the story of the deaths of Miriam and Aaron, the narrator shows how all that generation was coming to its end. It was soon to be time for a new generation to inherit God's promises and enter the land of Canaan.

— *Lessons from the Lawgiver's Life*

Moses' experience at Kadesh reveals the danger of anger. Moses' anger at Israel, possibly compounded by his grief at the death of his sister Miriam, drove him to identify Israel's anger at Yahweh with their anger at his own leadership. It was a common temptation, and one that would later tempt Samuel to equate Israel's rejection of Yahweh with their rejection of him (1 Sam. 8:6–7). Anger always distorts one's perception of reality, and so does not accomplish the righteousness of God (James 1:20). Throughout all his life from the days of his living in Egypt, Moses experienced the anger and rejection of his people, and after a lifetime of such opposition he had grown weary of it. All of his life he had listened to his people murmur and spread rumors that he was not to be trusted to keep his promise and lead Israel into a land of promised prosperity, and every difficulty Israel experienced along the way seemed to confirm this. It was not surprising

---

1   In Moses' challenge he demanded, "Shall we [i.e., he and Aaron] bring forth water for you from this rock?" Use of Aaron's staff also suggested Aaron agreed with the plan, and Yahweh's word of condemnation was spoken "to Moses and Aaron" (Num. 20:12).

that at every challenge their lack of faith in Moses and his brother Aaron (and their tribe of Levi) boiled to the surface.

At the end of almost forty years, after the death of his sister, Moses had enough of it. He therefore personalized their latest challenge, and used the opportunity to produce water from the rock to exalt himself in their eyes, forgetting that he was nothing, and that Yahweh was everything. Anger always blinds one and distorts what is before one's eyes. In his anger against his people, Moses used Yahweh's power to his own ends, to solidify his authority once and for all before his people. Aaron, who was easily swayed (compare this complicity in creating the golden bull calf and supporting his sister Miriam) joined with him in using this as an opportunity to cement their authority in Israel.

Yahweh's immediate response revealed their folly. Anger is usually always rooted in ego, and the servant of God must care nothing for his own reputation and only for the honor of his Lord. Moses should have realized that Israel's latest challenge concerned Yahweh alone, and not him or Aaron. All that mattered was exalting Yahweh by speaking serenely to the rock. Personalizing the contest was completely inappropriate, and striking the rock twice meant that he was striking not just the rocky crag, but Yahweh as well, since he was usurping His place as the leader of Israel.[1] It is not surprising that this act of anger resulted in Moses' forfeiture of his entry into the Promised Land, for that entry was conditional upon obedience.

Compare to 1 Cor. 10:4: "... the rock was Christ."

Day Thirty-Three

Grumbling near Edom: The Fiery Serpents

Prior to the death of Aaron, Israel attempted to pass through the land of Edom on their way to Moab and from there into the Promised Land. While still at Kadesh they sent messengers to the chieftain king of Moab, requesting with great diplomacy to allow them to pass through their land: "Please let us pass through your land. We will not pass through field or through vineyard; we will not even drink water from a well. We will go along the king's highway, not turning to the right or left until we pass through your territory" (Num. 20:17). The inhabitants of Edom therefore needn't fear that the large number of foreigners in their land would constitute a threat. They had not come to invade, and would not destroy or use up the local resources. They simply were passing through.

Nonetheless, the king of Edom did not believe them, refused them entry, and threatened military action if Israel entered their territory. Continued Israelite assurances that they were no threat and would pay whatever the locals charged for resources such as water accomplished nothing. The Edomites gathered a large military force to block their way. Israel had no choice but to go the long way around.

It was then that the people once more became impatient with Moses, renewing their old complaints, grumbling about the difficulties of finding food and water in the wilderness. They should never have left Egypt! Better to have remained there than to die here in the wilderness! They not only showed themselves ungrateful for their freedom from Egyptian slavery, but also ungrateful for the supernatural manna God unfailingly provided for them—concerning which they said, "We loathe this miserable food!"

Such ingratitude tried God's patience,[1] and in response He sent fiery serpents among them. They were called "fiery serpents" (literally, "a burner" in Num. 21:8) because its bite left a painful and fiery inflammation. (One suggestion is that the serpent in question was the highly poisonous and lethal carpet viper, found in Africa and the Middle East.) Many died from the infestation of snakes. So great was Israel's fear that they repented and sent a delegation to Moses, admitting they were wrong to complain and put God to the test, and asking him to intercede for them with Yahweh.

In response, as well as driving away the serpents, Yahweh did not simply grant healing to those who had been bitten, but commanded Moses to make a model of the fiery serpent out of copper and set it high up on a pole. Anyone who had been bitten, if they stared[2] at the pole, would find healing and be saved from death. It is possible that the pole was taken through the camp to allow those dying in their tents to stare at the pole with faith and so find recovery. In this way God granted Moses' request.

---

1   In 1 Cor. 10:9 St. Paul referred to their grumbling as "trying the Lord" [Greek ἐκπειράζω or *ekpeirazo*], "to put to the test," "tempt," "provoke."

2   The Hebrew word in Num. 21:9 often rendered "looked" is *nabat*, a different word than the usual word for looking or seeing, which is *ra'ah*.

— Lessons from the Lawgiver's Life

This story reveals to us the dangers that await us on the long journey through life. The narrator introduces the story by saying that the people "became impatient because of the journey"—i.e., because the way was long and hard, and it seemed as if the end was nowhere in sight. Such spiritual fatigue caused them to rebel against God and against Moses, even to the point of rejecting as worthless the divine gift of the bread of heaven. (No doubt the new roadblock set up by the king of Edom disheartened them even more.) Such discouragement brought on by life's inevitable trials can easily take the heart out of us—especially if we fail to look away from the trials and toward God. During such times of discouragement, we must look up from the road we travel and focus upon the Lord. He is the one who gives strength to the weary, and power to the weak. If we wait upon Him in prayer, though strong men tire and stumble, we will gain new strength. We will mount up with the wings of eagles; we will run and not be weary; we will walk and not faint (Isa. 40:29–31). If we fail to wait upon the Lord, like Israel we too will become impatient because of the journey, and may complain against the Lord.

This story also reveals to us the sacramental principle: God could have granted healing to the sick simple by fiat, or possibly made the healing conditional upon the afflicted person saying a prayer, but He did not. Rather, He made healing conditional upon their interaction with a physical object. God answered the prayer by commanding Moses to make a copper serpent and place it upon a pole so that it could be carried throughout the camp where the afflicted could interact with it.

We find this principle of using physical objects to convey spiritual power throughout God's dealings with Israel, beginning with Moses' use of his shepherd's rod as the instrument and conductor of divine power. In the same way, God used a tree as the instrument for healing the waters of Marah. Here again we find the same divine choice of a physical object to accomplish a spiritual work.

The nature of the object is significant as well. God could have decided to bring Moses' staff throughout the camp for the afflicted to behold, or any other physical object, but instead told Moses to craft a copper image of the very source of their danger and take that throughout the camp. It was as if the copper serpent on the pole drew to itself all the harm that the serpents had inflicted. The full and prophetic significance of the image would not be revealed until Christ came. As the serpent on the pole was lifted up in the wilderness as an image of death which nonetheless gave life to those who beheld it in faith, so too would Jesus be lifted up on the cross, a figure of death which also would give life to all who beheld Him in faith (John 3:14–15). The sacrament of the serpent became the salvation of the cross—the ultimate source of sacramental salvation for the whole world.

Day Thirty-Four
Victory over Sihon and Og

ISRAEL CONTINUED ITS PROGRESS toward the plains of Moab, where it would gather in preparation for its anticipated invasion of the Promised Land, across the Jordan River near to Jericho. As they had sent messengers to the king (or chieftain) of Edom asking to pass through his land, so they also sent messengers to Sihon the king (or chieftain) of the Amorites who lived in the land between the Arnon River in the south and the Jabbok River in the north. Sihon had his residence at Heshbon, and controlled the territory between the Arnon and Jabbok Rivers east of the Dead Sea and the Jordan River, an area about fifty miles from south to north.

Israel needed to pass through his land also, because that land stood between them and the plains of Moab to which they were heading. As they had before, they insisted that they simply wanted to use the road to pass through the land, and would not use or hurt any field or vineyard, nor drink water from any well. Whatever they needed they would purchase from the locals at the price they charged. Like the king of Edom, Sihon king of the Amorites refused Israel entry, but unlike the king of Edom, he was not content to simply prevent their entry, but used his soldiers to march out across the border and attack Israel. No doubt he considered this aggression justified as a defensive preemptive strike.

The battle was joined at Jahaz, a city on the eastern edge of Sihon's domains and north of the Arnon River. Sihon and his forces were soundly defeated by Israel, who put them to the edge of the sword, opening up the way there for eventual possession. Israel continued its advance northward to the plains of Moab, only to be confronted by yet another local chieftain king, Og, king of Bashan, who controlled land north of the Jabbok River. Og was something of a local terror, being himself a giant of a man. His "bed" or sarcophagus was of iron, and was nine cubits long—over thirteen feet! (One remembers the report of the spies who had been first sent out, and their declaration that giants lived in the Promised Land, compared to whom the Israelites were like grasshoppers.) Og and his forces marched out to drive Israel from his territory, and the two groups met at Edrei in the far north of the land, about thirty miles east of the Sea of Galilee.

God spoke to Moses before the battle, "Do not fear him, for I have given him into your hand, and all his people and all his land, and you shall do to them as you did to Sihon, king of the Amorites." Grasshoppers or not, Israel had Yahweh on their side, and they did not need to fear any giant or his armies. The people hearkened to Moses' assurance, and struck Og and his sons, and his forces, until none of his forces remained. Og and all his dynasty, and all the supporters who could rally in the future to threaten Israel must be eliminated if Israel was to survive. After their decisive defeat, Og's land also now lay open to Israel for eventual possession, and nothing now blocked their victorious march south to the plains of Moab east of the Jordan River and their eventual invasion of the Promised Land.

Though Sihon and Og were minor players in the geopolitical world of the ancient Near East compared to Egypt, they were the greatest forces Israel had yet fought, and they became archetypical of all their future mighty foes. We remember that the Israelite forces which gave battle against Sihon and Og were not professionally trained warriors like the kind of warriors that Egypt had. They did not have a great store of weaponry at their disposal, or even much experience of warfare, having spent all their adult lives as nomadic wanderers in the Sinai Peninsula. They had every reason, humanly speaking, to fear Sihon and Og, who had battle-hardened forces at their disposal, and who should have defeated the inexperienced Israelite nomads with no difficulty. But with God on their side, they won their battles against Sihon and Og in a decisive way, utterly destroying all opposition and leaving the way there clear for future expansion. The victories of Sihon and Og therefore became tokens and promises that they would win all their future battles once they invaded the Promised Land, provided only that they remained faithful and obedient to Yahweh.

That is why these early victories continued to be celebrated in song. Psalm 135 declared that God's power is manifested in the storms, and in His judgments on Pharaoh and the Egyptians, and also in Israel's victories over the mighty kings Sihon, king of the Amorites and Og, king of Bashan. So important were these early victories that the liturgical litany we find in Psalm 136 includes four strophes celebrating the victory over Sihon and Og. Yahweh not only made the heavens, and spread out the earth above the waters, and made the sun, moon, and stars, but He also "smote great kings and slew majestic kings, Sihon king of the Amorites and Og king of Bashan" (Ps. 136:17–20). In nature and in history alike, Yahweh reveals His power. And foremost in these manifestations of divine power, taking its place alongside Yahweh's victories over the Egyptian superpower, was the Israelite victory over the chieftains of the Canaanites of the Jordan valley in the first years of Israel's history when they fought under Moses' leadership.

— *Lessons from the Lawgiver's Life*

Israel's experience in the Transjordan reveals that warfare would be an essential part of Israel's future existence as a nation, just as warfare forms part of any nation's continued existence. This was especially true for Israel at the start of its national existence, since their existence involved the conquest and occupation of a territory filled with other people who were more technologically advanced and more heavily armed than they were. The Canaanite inhabitants of the land were not about to vacate simply because Yahweh, the god of another people, had somehow promised their land to the Hebrews recently liberated from Egypt. Israel would have to conquer Canaan in a long series of raids and wars, and then hold the land through armed vigilance. Their future warfare with and defeat by the Philistines showed that this was no easy matter.

In many ways, Israel's national existence was no different than that of the surrounding nations. All nations conducted wars upon their neighbors, and eventually empires would grow which were intent upon swallowing up many lesser nations. The willingness to make war and defend the national borders was the price everyone paid for their peace and security. Squeamish readers may take offense at the Bible's candid and unflinching approach to warfare, but the alternative to warfare and all that went with it was national extinction (which almost overtook Israel after their defeat at the hands of the Babylonians in 586 B.C.).

The transformation of the people of God from the nation of Israel to the trans-national Church brought with it a corresponding transformation of the warfare in which we as the people of God are to engage. The borders to be defended now are spiritual borders, meant to exclude error, not to keep out foreigners, and our enemies now are the spiritual enemies of demonic hosts, not the peoples of other nations. Though warfare for the people of God has become no longer military but spiritual, it is still as essential as ever for our survival. The forces of Sihon and Og were intent upon the defeat and annihilation of Israel, and in battle against them Israel could give no quarter. As Israel smote Sihon with the edge of the sword and smote Og and his sons and all his people until there was no was remnant left him (Num. 21:24, 35), so Christians must wage relentless warfare against Satan and sin. The weapons of our warfare are not physical, but spiritual. We now take as our target not the towers of Sihon and Og in the Transjordan, but godless speculations and every lofty thing raised against the knowledge of God (2 Cor. 10:4). No less than Israel of old, Christians are called upon by God to fight the foe.

Day Thirty-Five
Apostasy at Baal-Peor

AT LENGTH ISRAEL ARRIVED at the plains of Moab, east of the Jordan River across from Jericho. Shortly after they arrived there, they again fell into sin. At the same time as God was intervening on their behalf by refusing to allow Balaam, the diviner the Midianites of Moab had hired from afar, to curse them (Num. 22–24), Israel was once again beginning to rebel. The local Moabite women seduced the men of Israel, inviting them to join them in sacrificial feasts to the Moabite fertility god Baal, and to eventually intermarry with them—preceded, of course, by immediate sexual intercourse after the feast.

It seems as if the leaders of the people gave their consent to this acceptance of local hospitality, and even led the way in the apostasy. (It also seems that the work of the Moabite women was part of Balaam's strategy to infiltrate the Israelite camp and weaken their resolve to battle the local population; see Num. 31:15–16.) The men therefore left the camp, joined the local Moabite women in feasting and offering sacrifice to Baal, thereby pledging themselves to the foreign god.

So it was that "Israel joined themselves[1] to Baal of Peor, and Yahweh was angry with Israel" (Num. 25:3).

Even apart from the sexual aspect of their sin, their actions constituted a complete rejection of Yahweh and His covenant with them, for He had demanded their exclusive loyalty and specifically forbade such intermarriages, knowing they would lead to idolatrous syncretism. Yahweh's anger took the form of a plague which began to spread throughout the camp.

If the plague were to be halted, Israel must judicially punish the guilty parties with the penalty due to apostasy—i.e., death. Yahweh therefore commanded Moses to take the guilty leaders and hang them[2] before Yahweh under the sun—i.e., to execute them in broad daylight so that all the people would see and fear to repeat the offense. Moses passed along the order to the judges, the ones responsible for the administration of justice in Israel. As the news of the catastrophic sin and its required punishment spread throughout the camp, everyone began to weep, even up the doorway of the Tent of Meeting, expressing their grief had what had happened.

One young man, however, had no grief or contrition. His name was Zimri, son of Salu, who was a leader from the tribe of Simeon. That tribe was stationed nearby the Tent of Meeting, to its immediate south. It is probable that Salu, described as a leader, was among those whose execution was ordered by Moses, and that anger over the fate of his father drove Zimri in his defiance. Whatever his motivation, Zimri continued his course of sexual and spiritual rebellion against Yahweh, pointedly taking his Moabite woman (Cozbi by

---

1   The phrase "joined themselves" implies a continuing relationship with Baal, not a mere one night event. The LXX uses the verb τελειοω (*teleio*) the usual word used for consecratory initiation into a religion.

2   The LXX uses the verb παραδειγματίζω (*paradeigmatizo*), "to make a public example of" (compare the English word "paradigm").

name, daughter of an important Midianite chief) into the tent of himself and his brothers in full sight of Moses and everyone by the Tent of Meeting. By bringing her into the family tent, he was openly declaring his marriage to her.

This refusal to repent and to abide by the Law (e.g., Exod. 23:32–33) constituted a direct challenge, both to Yahweh's ruling and Moses' authority. He was publicly defying the religious exclusivity of Yahweh's Law and declaring that Israelites should be able to worship, marry, and join themselves to whichever deity or woman they chose.

One person seeing this defiant challenge was filled with zeal and indignation, and took immediate action. Phineas was from the priestly line, the grandson of Aaron; his name was Egyptian, and meant "dark skinned." Without waiting for the ordered executions of the leaders to be carried out, he took a spear and rushed into Zimri's family tent after him, entering the inner room of the tent. There he killed Zimri and his woman on the spot, "piercing both of them through, the man of Israel and the woman, through the belly" (Num. 25:8). This description indicates that both were killed by a single spear thrust—i.e., that he killed them while they were in the act of intercourse.[1] After this act of judicial justice, the plague stopped, even before any of the other guilty leaders had been executed. The damage had been bad: the text records that 24,000 died in the plague.[2] Israel's faithlessness (recorded in Num. 25) is contrasted with Yahweh's faithful-

---

1   This would explain why Zimri and Cozbi were in the "inner rooms" of the tent [Hebrew *qubba*]. Jerome in his Latin Vulgate rendered it as *lupanar*, "brothel," a meaning it can have in postbiblical Hebrew.

2   Regardless as to how this number is understood, the point is that the plague was so terrible that Phineas' zeal saved many others from joining the numbers of the dead. St. Paul makes the same point in 1 Cor. 10:8 when he wrote that "23,000 fell in one day" (with another 1,000 falling prey in the hours following the initial outbreak).

ness (recorded previously in Num. 22–24). Even at the end of their wilderness wandering and the beginning of their new life in Canaan, Israel remained a debtor to God's mercy.

— *Lessons from the Lawgiver's Life*

It was crucial for Israel's continued existence as the people of God set apart by Him to become a light to the world, that Israel not intermarry with the pagan nations surrounding them (thus the commands of Exod. 34:12–16; Deut. 7:3–4; Josh. 23:11–13), for such intermarriage would quickly lead to syncretistic idolatry. The integration into Israel of such people as Rahab and Ruth (Josh. 6:25; Ruth 4:11–14) shows that the issue was not race, but religion. Rahab and Ruth could join themselves to Israel and become a part of the covenant community, for the purity of the covenant would then still remain intact. That was entirely different from indiscriminate intermarriage, which resulted in tearing down the walls protecting covenant purity. At all costs Israel had to remain religiously separate from the idolatrous nations surrounding them, for Israel had a destiny culminating in the coming of the Messiah. Intermarriage threatened this saving separation.

In the same way Christians are forbidden to marry outside their faith. St. Paul allows a widow to remarry whomever she wishes—"only in the Lord" (1 Cor. 7:39). That is, she may only marry another Christian. Marrying an unbeliever is not an option. Mixed marriages of a Christian and a non-Christian are tolerated as inevitable, since sometimes after two non-Christians marry, only one of them converts to Christ. But no Christian may voluntarily contract a marriage to a non-Christian. In Orthodox canonical practice, doing so places the Christian spouse outside the Church.

This is not an arbitrary rule. For Christians, marriage is about Christ, since everything in life is about Him. As a Christian strives to serve Christ in every part of life, so he or she must strive to serve Him in their marriage as well, mak-

ing the marriage one more way of serving Him, and as a ve-
hicle for His glory. But marriage can only function in this
way when both partners know the Lord. A Christian who
knowingly marries an unbeliever thereby makes a decision
to exclude that marriage from Christ's influence, and to
wall off an important and central part of their life from the
Lord. No wonder the Church forbids such a thing. We must
open all parts of our life to Christ, especially our marriage,
and ask that He make it an instrument for His glory in the
world. Like Israel of old, the intermarriage of the people of
God with those who do not serve Israel's God is categorically
forbidden.

Day Thirty-Six
The War on Midian

T HE MIDIANITES WERE CLEARLY a danger to Israel.
They had hired Balaam to come from far away at great
cost to curse Israel (even though Yahweh moved him
to bless Israel instead), and they had been part of Balaam's
strategy to use the adult Moabite women among them to se-
duce Israel and weaken them. Moses therefore declared them
a national enemy, and put them under the ban—that is, they
were the objects of holy war, and no treaty could be made
with them even if they were willing to surrender. They were
to be devoted to destruction: "Be hostile to the Midianites
and strike them, for they have been hostile to you with their
schemes" (Num. 25:17–18).

After a military census of Israelite warriors had been accomplished, the time came for Israel to counterattack Midian. Yahweh gave Moses the order: "Take full vengeance for
the sons of Israel on the Midianites. Afterward you will be
gathered to your people" (Num. 31:2). This was to be Moses'
final battle before his time came to die.

A thousand were chosen from each of the twelve tribes[1]
and they went out to battle along with Phineas the priest
and the holy vessels, for this was holy war, not any ordinary
military skirmish. With God in their midst they were vic-

---

1   Possibly meaning twelve military units in all.

torious, and according to the rules for holy war, they killed every male they found. That included the kings or chieftains of Midian, and the famous trouble maker Balaam. They took all the women and the children as part of the plunder, along with flocks and herds, and returned to the base camp at the plains of Moab.

Keeping alive the adult women, however, was in clear violation of the rules for holy war, which declared that all adults be put to the sword. No doubt they argued that the women were no danger to them—an idea of which Moses quickly disabused them! "Have you spared the women? Behold these caused the sons of Israel, through the word of Balaam, to defect from Yahweh, so the plague was among Yahweh's congregation!" These adult women were not harmless as they thought, but must be put to the sword as were the men, though the young girls could be spared, to be raised as part of the covenant community. That was how warfare worked in the ancient world, and holy war in particular (see Ps. 137:9, which provides a glimpse of the ancient practice of war).

The sacred text then exults in declaring the tremendous amount of plunder taken, including sheep, cattle, donkeys, and much gold. This was divided among all the people, including the Levites, who had no inheritance allotted in the Promised Land. The tremendous amount of plunder taken expresses the greatness of the victory which Yahweh had given them. The meticulous totaling up of the plunder is intended to express Yahweh's provision for His covenant people when they obey Him courageously on the field of battle and trust Him for victory.

Many people find accounts like this troubling to modern sensitivities. It is important therefore to remember that we are reading an ancient text, and one that presupposes moral norms of the ancient world. In that world, taking plunder in war was the norm, and was often the only payment that soldiers received for risking their lives on the field of battle. That plunder including taking the defeated foe as slaves, and executing all the male combatants and their male children (who could later arise to avenge their fathers if left alive).

The Law's acceptance of slavery as a normal part of the world should not be read as God's timeless blessing of slavery. Like divorce, slavery was left intact by the Law "due to the hardness of men's hearts" (see Matt. 19:8), to be dealt with and changed at the proper time. The provisions of the Law presuppose Bronze Age cultural norms, which could not be uprooted and overturned all at once. St. Paul recognized the temporary and provisional character of the Law when he declared that it was but a tutor to bring us to Christ (Gal. 3:24).

Lessons from the Lawgiver's Life

The account of the aftermath of the victorious war against the Midianites offers two lessons for those engaged in spiritual warfare against sin and passions.

The first lesson regards the execution of the Midianite women. The Israelite warriors initially judged that these adult Midianite women would be no threat to their future security, and declined to execute them as they waged holy war. Moses recognized, based on the women's proven past actions, that they could not be trusted, and indeed would prove to be a threat in the future. Accordingly, they too must be put under the ban along with their men. This story tells us of the danger of leaving certain sinful passions in our life. The abiding temptation is to label certain sins as "unacceptable" with the result that we try to uproot them, and certain other lesser sins as "acceptable" with the result that we decline to uproot them.

In fact, all sin will eventually prove lethal to our spiritual life eventually. Sins are like cancerous cells—their size is unimportant. If left alone, they will grow, spread, and finally bring death. St. James warned of this: "When sin is full grown, it brings forth death" (James 1:15). George MacDonald said the same: "There is no heaven with a little hell in it—

no plan to retain this or that of the devil in our heart or our pockets. Out Satan must go, every hair and feather."[1] There can be no acceptable sin, no treaty made with the devil. Our opposition to sin in our lives must be total and relentless. The battle will be hard and long, and will last our whole life into the time when we cross over into the next life. But we must never settle for less than complete victory. There must be no retreat, no surrender—and no compromise with what would ultimately destroy us.

The second lesson regards the tremendous amount of plunder gathered after the victory. If our battle is a spiritual one against the forces of sin and death, then the plunder gained after victory is spiritual as well. We fight not to gain sheep, cattle, and gold, but the spiritual riches of joy, serenity, and immortality. Too often our lives are filled with grief, turmoil, worry, and fear. As we continue to gain victory over the passions, these are replaced the fruit of the Spirit, and we increasingly amass the spiritual wealth that enriches our lives and makes us radiant with the presence of Christ. It is for these riches that we fight on, and persevere, and refuse to heed the wounds. The spiritual riches available in Christ even in this life are worth the pain and noise of battle.

1   George MacDonald, *Unspoken Sermons*, "The Last Farthing," (London: Longmans, Green & Co. , 1886) 103.

Part Four

THE SEVERE MERCY

Day Thirty-Seven
The Refused Request

AFTER THESE PROMISING victories in the Transjordan, Moses knew that his own life would soon be over. Though he was still in comparatively good health, he was after all 120 years old. All of his long life, since his youthful and (foolishly zealous) days in Egypt, he had yearned for his ancestral people to be free of the Egyptian yoke and living at peace in the land God had promised to their forefathers. How many times had he fallen asleep at night, longing to enter that good land, and imagining what it would be like to finally be there? He had promised the fulfillment of this dream to Israel over and over again from their days spent under Pharaoh's lash.

Crossing the Jordan and inheriting that promise was the goal of his entire life. Since he had first left Egypt as a wanted fugitive and found a haven in the land of Midian among the tents of Reuel, his life had been that of a humble nomad. He longed to call some place home. It could no longer be in Egypt with the family with which he grew up. Now it could only be in the land God promised to his forefathers, the good land flowing with milk and honey, the land into which Moses constantly had promised he would lead his people if only they would obey him and trust their God. Doubtless he often imagined himself leading them home in triumph, crossing the Jordan, winning the battles in Canaan which the spies he had sent had foolishly refused to wage forty years earlier. Then at last he could settle down in peace and finally enjoy the promised reward with his people.

We can therefore begin to glimpse the depth of his pain at being refused it. After Moses broke faith with God at the Meribah rock of Kadesh, God had declared that in punishment for this, Moses would not enter the Promised Land with the rest of the people. Instead, it was Joshua who would lead Israel across the Jordan into Canaan. Moses, God told him, was soon to ascend the mountains of Abarim[1] and see the Promised Land from afar, after which he would be gathered to his people in death.

Perhaps, Moses thought, given the tremendous patience and forgiveness that Yahweh had extended to Israel over and over again throughout the decades, He would grant him forgiveness of his sin also. After all, he had only broke faith once, while Israel had rebelled constantly. Therefore, heartbroken and unable to bear the thought of being denied entry into Canaan after so many sacrifices and after so many years, Moses made bold to ask Yahweh to change His mind.

Moses therefore decided to ask God to pardon his sin and allow him to enter Canaan after all. Yahweh had begun to give Israel victory over their foes in the Transjordan, and Moses couldn't bear the thought of missing the victories to come. He prayed, "O Lord Yahweh, You have only begun to show Your servant Your greatness and Your powerful hand. What god is there in heaven or on the earth who does deeds and mighty acts like Yours? Please let me cross over so that I may see the good land which is beyond the Jordan" (Deut. 3:24–25). After God had extended undeserved forgiveness to Israel so many times, surely He would forgive His own

---

1   That is, the mountain range on the western border of Moab where they were—more specifically, Mount Nebo (Deut. 34:1).

faithful servant this once?

It was not to be. The request was vigorously rejected and refused. In fact Yahweh reacted with anger to the request. He cut Moses short, and said, "That is enough! Speak to Me no more about this! Go up to the summit of Pisgah and raise your eyes toward the west and the north and the south and the east, and look with your eyes, for you will not cross over this Jordan. But charge Joshua, and encourage and strengthen him, for he shall go over at the head of this people, and shall put them in possession of the land which you shall see." That was the end of it. His young aide, Joshua, would take over, and would inherit the land that he was only allowed to see from afar. Moses would pay for his sin in full; Yahweh would not relent or change His mind.

— Lessons from the Lawgiver's Life

Surveying the larger canvas of the conquest of Canaan and seeing how Moses was unable to enter the Promised Land, and how the land would be conquered under the leadership of Joshua, we can learn a lesson with the tools of typology and allegory.

The Promised Land has always been an image of our final heavenly rest. In Hebrews 4:1–10 we find the rest that Israel obtained in the land of Canaan used as an image of the soul's final rest in heaven after the labors of this life. Even the old spiritual hymn "Michael Row the Boat Ashore" contains an image of the archangel Michael rowing our soul across the cold Jordan River of death to a land of milk and honey on the other side. Given this, it becomes typologically significant that Moses the Lawgiver was not able to lead the people of God into their promised inheritance, for human effort alone is not sufficient to bring us into the Kingdom. The Law, used as an instrument of human striving to gain merit or earn salvation, cannot save. Moses, understood allegorically as an embodiment of the Law and of human striving, is unable to lead us to our final goal, for our best efforts are always marred by sin. Whether it was Moses at the waters of Meribah in Kadesh or ourselves at many places in our lives, our rebellion against God provokes the just penalty of exclusion from His presence.

In this story of Moses' inability to lead Israel into the Promised Land, we read that the one who leads them into Canaan instead of Moses is Joshua. His original name was "Hoshea" (Hebrew for "he saved" or "he rescued"), but in Numbers 13:16 Moses changed it to "Joshua" (Hebrew for "Yahweh saves" or "Yahweh rescues"). It cannot be coincidental that this is the same name given to the Savior, the son of Mary (Matt. 1:21; Luke 1:31). In Hebrew, the name is Yehoshua (or "Yeshua"), which in Greek is rendered Ἰησοῦς or *Iesous*, and in English "Jesus." (see chapter 16 above.) Thus it is not Moses who leads the people of God into their final rest, but Joshua; it is not our striving to keep the Law of Moses or to earn God's love which leads us to our final salvation, but Jesus and the mercy which flows from His cross.

Moses' failure therefore points to our own failures, and his inability to enter the Promised Land points to the insufficiency of our own efforts to save ourselves. It is only through Yeshua the Savior that we can find salvation, and enter the heavenly rest.

Day Thirty-Eight
Renewing the Covenant

FINALLY, IN THE ELEVENTH month of the fortieth year after Israel left Egypt, Moses addressed his people as they waited on the plains of Moab to begin their long-delayed invasion of the Promised Land. It was important that Israel know the magnitude of their previous sins and of their present debt to Yahweh, and so Moses rehearsed for them again the history of their doings since they left Horeb as the newly-covenanted people of God. Only by knowing what Yahweh had done for their fathers and themselves could they truly rededicate themselves to the service of Yahweh as they began a new life as His holy people in Canaan. Moses' long address took the basic form of the covenant treaties common at that time, agreements which a Hittite king might make with his vassal, for Israel was again called to renew their covenant with Yahweh, their king.

These treaties began with a historical prologue, rehearsing the benefits that the king had bestowed upon his vassal, which was followed by the basic terms of the treaty, and then by further details and treaty stipulations. The gods of the various parties were then invoked as witnesses to watch over them to judge and punish violations of the treaty. Blessings for keeping the covenant treaty then were detailed, as

well as curses for breaking the treaty.[1] The text of the treaty
was deposited in a sacred archive so that future generations
might refer to it as necessary. Provisions were also made for a
public reading of the treaty at least once a generation.[2] It was
this basic treaty structure that provided the outline for Moses' address for the renewal of the covenant. Obviously, some
variations to the pattern had to be made, for no other gods
could be invoked as witnesses. In their place, Moses called
upon heaven and earth to witness what Israel was agreeing to,
as well as the written record of the Law itself (Deut. 30:19,
20; 31:26).[3]

Following this pattern, Moses therefore gathered Israel
together to repeat to them by way of historical prologue the
sins their fathers committed a generation before, which resulted in those lost and wasted years wandering about the
wilderness. He recounted their recent victories in the Transjordan and how God had cared for them from the days of
their liberation from Egypt until now. He then repeated for
them the basic stipulations of the covenant: the Ten Words
and their obligation to love and worship Yahweh alone. Then
followed a repetition of the detailed stipulations of the covenant, including the many laws God had given them (contained in Deut. 12-26).

Moses also told them that when Israel finally passed over
the Jordan River, they must renew their covenant with Yahweh in the Promised Land, building an altar there and offering sacrifice. They must write the words of the Law on stones
plastered with lime. Six of the tribes must stand on Mount
Ebal near Shechem where the stones were, and the other six
tribes opposite on Mount Gerizim, with the Levites bearing the Ark in the middle. Those Levites would announce

---

1   Compare the blessings and curses in Deut. 28:1–14 and 15–58.
2   Compare such provisions in Deut. 31:26 and 31:9–13.
3   In a later renewal ceremony Joshua would invoke the stone which
     had been set up nearby as a witness (Josh. 24:26–27).

the curses and blessings of the covenant, and all the people would respond "Amen," thereby agreeing to keep the covenant. Having given Israel these liturgical instructions for use after they crossed the Jordan, Moses concluded by detailing the blessings and curses that would overtake them in the case of obedience or disobedience.

Moses' address to Israel, though broadly patterned after the treaties of that day, was not simply the terms of an agreement to which Israel was agreeing. It was a final impassioned heartfelt plea for them to cease their rebellious ways once and for all and to love their God. Over and over again, in both the historical prologue recounting Yahweh's patient care and throughout the repetition of the terms of the covenant law itself, Moses stressed how great was the privilege to which Yahweh was admitting them. Through Yahweh's care and His faithfulness to their forefathers, Israel was "a holy people...Yahweh your God has chosen you to be a people for Himself, a special treasure above all the peoples on the face of the earth" (Deut. 7:6).

With such a privilege went the sacred obligation to cleave to Yahweh alone, uttering abhorring the worship of other gods and refusing to assimilate with the peoples around them. Obedience was critical, and they must take care to teach their children at every opportunity that they must love Yahweh alone.

Moses knew only too clearly that a rebellious streak remained in the hearts of the people—as the recent affair of idolatry with the Baal of Peor demonstrated only too well. Their victories in the Transjordan over Sihon and Og might have given Israel a false sense of security, leading them to imagine that they were the source of their victories, and that their military strength would inevitably continue after they crossed the Jordan into the Promised Land. It was too easy for Israel to reconfigure Yahweh so that He resembled the gods of the other nations, and to think of religion in merely transactional terms; yet, if they sacrificed to Yahweh alone,

He would repay them with victory and blessing.

Moses knew that Yahweh wanted more than mere sacrifice—He wanted their hearts, their love, their devotion. At the core of the covenant was a call to relationship: "Hear, O Israel! Yahweh is our God, Yahweh alone! You shall love Yahweh your God with all your heart, with all your soul, and with all your strength" (Deut. 6:4–5). In a long emotional address, Moses pleaded with his people one last time to cleave to God, knowing that He was their life.

In this long exhortation, we see the heart of the Law revealed. Despite the many detailed laws, legal rulings, and judicial guidance given which Israel would need to govern their daily life in Canaan, the mystical element still shines through. At its center and core, Mosaic religion was not primarily about law and jurisprudence, but about communion with the living God. Yahweh had come to dwell in their midst that He might bless them. He had established the liturgical cult of ark, altar, shrine, and sanctuary so that, living among them as the consuming fire, they would not be consumed. At the center of their life stood an altar, not a book. The book was given (in that overwhelmingly oral culture) as the archive for the priests so that the people could learn what sort of lives Yahweh expected from His people. Only so could they be blessed by Him as they drew near to sacrifice and commune.

— *Lessons from the Lawgiver's Life*

During their wilderness wandering, all the tribes had been arranged around the Ark in the same way that the troops of an army in the field were arranged around their king. That arrangement would in some measure continue when they reached the Promised Land. The tribes would no longer all live together in one single camp, but would be scattered throughout the land in their allotted cities and villages. But Yahweh would still live among them nonetheless, as the portable shrine encamped in their midst (and moved from place to place, as needed), forming their spiritual center of gravity. In whatever city or village they lived, they would still all resort to Yahweh at His Tent of Meeting three times a year (e.g., Deut. 12:5; 16:16). The centrality of the Ark not only gave the tribes their unity. It also revealed that what God wanted was mystical communion. This is the main lesson we may learn from this event in the life of Moses the lawgiver.

Day Thirty-Nine
The Death of Moses: A Song, a Blessing, and an Ascent

A Song

AT THE CONCLUSION of Moses' long exhortation to the people preparing them to enter Canaan and into formal covenant with Yahweh at the ceremony by Mount Ebal and Mount Gerazim, he knew that their hearts still harbored rebelliousness against Yahweh and that judgment would fall upon them in the Promised Land. Yahweh had clearly told him so, and He gave Moses a song to teach Israel to help keep them in the right way and to direct them whenever they strayed: "Write this song and teach it to the people of Israel; put it in their mouths, that this song may be a witness for Me against the people of Israel. And when many evils and troubles have come upon them, this song shall confront them as a witness" (Deut. 31:19).

The song was a long hymn praising Yahweh's faithfulness, as well as Israel's apostasy, punishment, and repentant return to God. Moses taught it to them as a kind of national anthem, a folk song to be embedded in their culture, warning them of the dangers of apostasy and of the willingness of their God to restore them when they returned to Him. It was a brilliant strategy, akin to enshrining an antiracist song like Dylan's Blowin' in the Wind in a culture given to racism. The Song of Moses (Deut. 32) describes the apostasy of Israel and their resultant punishment from God, as well as God's desire to bless Israel when they returned to obedience. It constituted a kind of protest song, protesting in advance their tendency to apostasy and rebellion. Moses would soon not be there to rebuke Israel for their backsliding, but his song would abide and speak to them.

A Blessing

On the very day that Moses taught Israel this song, God told him that it was time ascend Mount Nebo to die. He therefore turned to his ancestral people for whom he had suffered so much to give them a final blessing. In it he blessed the tribes one by one, invoking God's mercy upon them in a spirit of prophecy (Deut. 33). In offering a dying man's benediction Moses was not simply expressing a pious wish, but effectively bringing divine blessing upon the people of God. Like Jacob before him (Gen. 49), Moses exercised his fatherly authority over the twelve sons or tribes of Israel, commending them to their covenant God.

In this benediction, Moses revealed not only God's majesty and power to bless His people, but his own heart as well. Despite the many times they opposed him and rebelled against his authority, even to the point of wanting to stone him, Moses still loved his people. He would not die without giving them a final blessing. There is no record in the Bible of Moses being commanded by God to bless Israel before ascending Mount Nebo to die. It seems as if the final blessing came from his own great heart.

An Ascent

After blessing his people, Moses went up from the plains of Moab to Mount Nebo, which is opposite Jericho across the

Jordan River, and God showed him all the land. The divine commentary must have been heartbreaking as Moses surveyed the land, all of which he could see from the height of Nebo: "This is the land which I swore to give to Abraham, to Isaac, and to Jacob. I have let you see it with your eyes, but you shall not go there" (Deut. 34:4). The Biblical account is succinct: "So Moses the servant of Yahweh died there in the land of Moab, according to the word of Yahweh" (v. 5). Moses' humility and his servant's heart shines through the Biblical text, for it records not a word of reply on the part of Moses, nor a single murmur of protest. Yahweh gave him one final command, and he obeyed, stepping from this world into the next.

Normally a man's family would be responsible for the burial, in this case his surviving spouses and children. But not here. Such was Moses' closeness to Yahweh that Yahweh stepped in and performed the office of the family: "He [presumably Yahweh, the only other grammatical antecedent] buried him in the valley in the land of Moab opposite Beth-peor, but no man knows the place of his burial to this day" (Deut. 34:6).[1] This is the only instance in all Scripture where God Himself buried the body of one of His servants. It reveals as nothing else could God's love for Moses, His faithful servant and man of God. In the culture of his day, Moses' burial was the responsibility of his siblings, Aaron or (in event of his death), perhaps Miriam. Since they had predeceased him, God decided that He would assume that responsibility, performing the part normally played by Moses' brother. Yahweh had always declared that Moses was different than others, for He spoke with Moses "face to face," as a man speaks with his friend and brother. God allowed no one

---

1   One assumes that after ascending the mountain to die, Joshua and others later followed him there to bury him, only to find no trace of him or his grave, so that they concluded God had buried him in a place nearby the camp in the valley of Moab.

else the privilege of burying His beloved friend; that duty of kinship belonged to Him alone.

A Severe Mercy

Given God's great love for Moses, one cannot help but ask why God refused to pardon his sin and refuse him entry into the Promised Land. Why such severity toward Moses when so much mercy and indulgence had been shown to Israel? In questions such as this we approach a great mystery, and can only offer a guess. But it is a guess consistent with other teachings of Scripture.

In 1 Cor. 11:17ff. we find a discussion of sin and the Lord's Supper. In this discussion, Paul refers to those who eat the Eucharistic bread and cup unworthily, thereby eating and drinking not salvation, but judgment. This judgment consisted of sickness and even death—"That is why many of you are weak and sick, and some have died" (1 Cor. 11:30). Then Paul adds, "But when we are judged by the Lord, we are disciplined, so that we may not be condemned along with the world" (v. 32). It seems that the Lord judged these Corinthian Christians severely with sickness and death in this life, to spare them the worse judgment of eternal condemnation which the godless world would experience.

— *Lessons from the Lawgiver's Life*

In the same way, I suggest that those who are of God's "household" (cf. 1 Pt. 4:17) are subjected to more stringent judgment in this age to spare them from the judgment in the age to come.[1] Conversely, those who have rejected God in this life are sometimes spared stringent judgment in this age, for God has delayed their judgment until the age to come—to

---

1   Cf. 1 Pet. 4:17.

their greater condemnation.[1] In this regard one cannot help but think of the bishops who persecuted and hounded St. John Chrysostom to his death—nothing terrible happened to them in this age. They finished their lives in honor and did not pay for their sins in this life. It would seem that such was the gravity of their sin that God reserved the entirety of judgment of their sin to the age to come, where the judgment would be the more severe.

If this is the way God deals with sin in this age, then one can see how God dealt with Moses' sin with a severe mercy. Because Moses was God's esteemed and favored servant, God dealt with all of his sins in this age, judging them here by denying him entry into the Promised Land. That means that the debt owed to God for his sin was completely paid for in this age, and that no outstanding debt was left to the age to come. The apparent severity of God's judgment here in this life therefore concealed God's mercy. Moses was judged by the Lord while in Moab and experienced His discipline there that he might be spared further judgment in the age to come. Moses passed from this world with little left to judge in the world to come—a severe mercy, but a mercy indeed!

---

1   The human mind can be easily overwhelmed in trying to grasp the paradoxical nature of God's mercy and judgment. The author's intent here is to encourage us to trust that, though we be judged severely in this life, this judgment is evidence of God's chastening love (cf. Heb. 12:6). —Eds.

Day Forty

"The Law was given through Moses"

The Excellence of the Law

IT IS TRUE THAT COMPARED to the glory of Christ that shines in the life of one illumined by the Spirit, the glory of the Mosaic Law shines but dimly, and that the glory of the New Covenant surpasses that of the Old Covenant (2 Cor. 3:7–11). But this truth should not make us forget that until Christ came, the Law that Moses received shone as the light of the world. In a world of idols and demons, it revealed the true and living God; in a world which had lost his way, it pointed the way home; in a world of moral chaos and confusion, it provided the only moral compass then available. The Law that Moses received on Mount Sinai was luminous, disinfectant; it revived the weary soul, gave wisdom to the simple (Ps. 19:7). In an age in which every man did what was right in his own eyes and no certainty was possible, in a world where everyone found themselves sinking in a moral quagmire, the Law was the only solid rock around, the only light this world afforded.

In a word, the Law was the cultural Bronze Age expression of the timeless wisdom of God. Baruch 3:36–4:4 sums it up very well: "God found the whole way to knowledge and gave her [i.e., wisdom] to Jacob His servant and to Israel whom He loved. Afterward she appeared upon earth and lived among men. She is the book of the commandments of God and the Law that endures forever. Turn, O Jacob, and take her; walk toward the shining of her light. Happy are we, O Israel, for we know what is pleasing to God!"

The Law revealed the heart of God and what He wanted from His people. In particular, it revealed that God delighted in justice, compassion, sexual purity, fidelity, truthfulness, and loyalty. More than anything, it revealed that He wanted faithfulness and love from the creatures He had made. He was patient and kind, and delighted to liberate and bless. His sovereignty and power were boundless; He needed nothing, and He Himself provided all that His creatures would ever need. Israel's privileged place among the nations was never intended as an end in itself: Israel was given its privileged place so that it could reveal God to the rest of the world, and become a light to those in darkness (Rom. 2:18–20).

The Excellence of the Lawgiver

Given the excellence of the Law, we can more easily see the excellence God required in the one he chose to receive this Law. If the Levites had to be holy to bear the Ark, how much more did the Lawgiver have to be holy to receive the Law!

This is why we can look to Moses as a great exemplar for those seeking to please God. Moses embodied the qualities which were expressed in the Law he received.

Moses was courageous. For courage is not the absence of fear, but a willingness to do the right thing in the face of fear. Moses naturally (and quite sensibly) feared the wrath of Pharaoh, which is why he fled from Egypt in the first place. He knew only too well his weakness and lack of experience on the international stage, and feared to return to Egypt to challenge Pharaoh. Yet he finally returned to Egypt nonetheless, facing down the superpower of his day and defying Pharaoh to his face. When confronted with onrushing Egyptian chariots at the Red Sea, or the daunting desert of the Sinai Peninsula, or the rebellious crowds intent upon stoning him in the wilderness, Moses' courage never faltered.

Moses was humble. That is, he relied entirely upon Yahweh, trusting in His word. He never used his authority over his people to enrich himself at their expense, not even taking from them a single donkey (Num. 16:15).

Moses was compassionate and self-sacrificing. Despite the constant opposition that he received and despite his being the target of grumbling and discontent for forty years from his fellow Israelites, he interceded for them every time they were in need. When Yahweh's wrath justly flared up against Israel and when He threatened to destroy them, Moses always threw himself down before God to beg undeserved mercy for them. Indeed, Moses was even willing to forfeit his own place in the book of God's favor if this would save his people. Moses repaid the evil he received from Israel with good throughout his life.

Finally, Moses was, with the exception of a single time, obedient to the commands of God. The loving obedience that God in His Law required from His people found embodiment in the life of the Lawgiver. From the time that Moses reentered Egypt to the time he ascended Mount Nebo to die, he revealed what a life of faithfulness to God looked like. Though living in the Bronze Age Middle East, he became a man for all seasons in his obedience to God.

The Lawgiver and Jesus Christ

In John 1:17, we read that "the Law was given through Moses; grace and truth came through Jesus Christ." One might imagine therefore that Moses never met Jesus Christ, and in one sense this is true, for Moses lived and died in about the thirteenth century BC, many centuries before Mary gave birth to her son in Bethlehem. But the Gospel record reveals that Moses did meet Jesus after his death on Mount Nebo.

At Christ's Transfiguration on Mount Tabor, He spoke to Moses, the great Lawgiver and embodiment of the Law, and to Elijah, the great prophet and embodiment of the prophets. Together, Moses and Elijah represented the Law and the prophets, the Hebrew Scriptures as a whole; that is, the Law and the Prophets, the Hebrew Scriptures, looked forward to Jesus and found their fulfillment in Him. Jesus was not just another prophet like Moses, Isaiah, Jeremiah, or Elijah, standing at the end of their long line. He was their fulfillment, the goal to which all that came before Him were heading.

Significantly, when Moses conversed with Jesus at His Transfiguration, they were discussing Jesus' own exodus, His departure, the exit that He would make from this life on the Cross (Luke 9:31).[1] Moses' exodus formed the center of his life, and so did the exodus of Jesus.

But, I suggest, a deeper christological reading of the Old Testament will reveal a deeper connection of Moses with Jesus. For Christians, the Father always reveals Himself through His Son, His eternal Logos. No one can see God the Father at any time; it is through His eternal Word that He is made known (John 1:18). Thus, in the Old Testament, every time Yahweh, God the Father, made Himself known in theophany, He made Himself known through His eternal Logos and Word. All the manifestations of Yahweh in the Old Testament were indeed manifestations of God the Father, but they were also manifestations of the Holy Trinity, for the Father always only manifested Himself through His Son by the Holy Spirit.

Thus, when Yahweh manifested Himself to Isaiah in the Temple so that Isaiah declared, "I saw the Lord sitting upon a throne, high and exalted" and when he said that "my eyes have seen the King, Yahweh of hosts" (Isa. 6:1, 5), this was

---

[1] Luke 9:31 says that they "spoke of His departure" [Greek Ἔξοδος or *exodos*] which He was about to fulfill at Jerusalem."

vision of the pre-incarnate Word. That is why John said of this vision, "Isaiah saw His glory [i.e., the glory of Jesus] and spoke about Him" (John 12:41).

This being so, it is clear that the God who called Moses from the burning bush and revealed Himself to Moses as the eternal "I Am" was the pre-incarnate Word. Christ confirmed this when He confronted His adversaries and declared, "Amen, amen, I say to you, before Abraham was born, I Am" (John 8:58). Here Christ was explicitly claiming to be the I Am who revealed Himself to Moses at the burning bush. No wonder His foes picked up stones to stone Him for blasphemy.

The connection that Moses had with Christ therefore was as intimate a connection as could be imagined. Christ, the pre-incarnate Word, Yahweh before the ages, was the one who revealed Himself to Moses at the burning bush, and the one by whose power Moses parted the Red Sea. Christ was the one who led him through the wilderness in the pillar of cloud and fire. Christ was the one who finally buried Moses in the valley in the land of Moab. Moses, in his final song, declared that Yahweh was the Rock whose work was perfect and whose ways were justice (Deut. 32:4). Indeed, He was. This Rock accompanied Moses and his people throughout their long wilderness wandering, providing them with spiritual food and drink, "and the Rock was Christ" (1 Cor. 10:3–4).

— *Lessons from the Lawgiver's Life*

Our day is in great need of moral examples. In a day of moral cowardice when many are too afraid to stand up against the forces of secularism and sin, we need an example of courage. In a day of swollen hubris when our culture exults in its military might and imagines that such might entitles it to force its will upon other nations, we need an example of humility. In a day of selfishness when many choose their own luxurious comfort over the welfare and lives of the helpless (including the poor and the helpless unborn), we need an example of compassion and self-sacrifice. In a day of rebellion when moral restraint and accountability have been thrown off and tradition trampled, we need an example of godly obedience. Fortunately for us, we have such an example. It is Moses, the man of God.

The End